Praise for the nationally bestselling

Life in Motion
An Unlikely Ballerina

"Wrenching and revelatory."

—*The New York Times*

"An unexpected page turner . . . Her story is an inspiration to anyone—man or woman, black or white—who has ever chased a dream against the odds, and the grace with which she triumphs is an example for us all."

—*Booklist* (starred review)

"Thorough, sensitive . . . clear-eyed."

—*The Washington Post*

"Reads as a modern-day Cinderella story . . . this memoir is an inspirational read—especially for aspiring dancers."

—*Jet* magazine

"[A] dramatic rags-to-toe-shoes life story."

—*People*

"Her path to becoming a star ballerina has been as dramatic, unlikely, and hinged on coincidence as the plots of most ballets."

—Rivka Galchen, *The New Yorker*

"[*Life in Motion*] reveals a woman as graceful and powerful in life as she is in dance."

—Melissa Harris Perry

"[Parts] the curtain on the ballet's central illusion: that it is empowering for the female dancers at its centre. Providing a behind-the-scenes look at the glory and gore of ballet. . . . You find yourself rooting for her."

—Deidre Kelly, *The Globe and Mail* (Canada)

"Remarkable."

—*Juicy* magazine

"Engaging . . . [Copeland is] a poised, intelligent writer whose temperament—disciplined, determined, driven—gives the book a special spark. . . . In *Life in Motion*, she looks back on the past without bitterness or anger, only gratitude. Hers is an out-of-the-ordinary story about defying stereotypes, and she shares it in an inspiring narrative that's enlivened by her own grace and generous spirit."

—*BookPage*

"It's no wonder Misty Copeland is a role model for countless aspiring ballerinas."

—*Dance Spirit Magazine*

"A gift to all balletomanes, not just the brown ones."

—Esther Cepeda

"A wonderful read."

—Jia Tolentino, *The Hairpin*

"Misty Copeland, a ballerina of extraordinary talent and charisma, offers an autobiography as mesmeric as her dancing. She overcame adversity in the studio, in her home life, and in ballet's own traditionalism to become one of its brightest stars —her passion and perseverance will inspire dancers and nondancers alike."

—Eliza Minden, author of *The Ballet Companion* and cofounder and head of design at dancewear company Gaynor Minden, Inc.

"A raw, honest tale of growing up and into the calling of a lifetime. . . . Her memoir is filled with passion, pain, success, and . . . pure joy."

—*Ebony*

"Misty's unwavering belief that we can be anything that we dream is an inspiration—an inspiration to break the mold, follow your passion, never take no for an answer, and do it all with grace, kindness and the spirit to help others on their journey. I am thrilled that my two daughters have a role model in Misty, who is breaking down doors that that they will never have to."

—Rachel Roy, fashion designer

"Misty Copeland's *Life in Motion* is an inspiration to all young people. She is the Jackie Robinson of the ballet world, and a true role model for an entire generation of new ballerinas."

—Frank Sanchez, vice president,
Boys & Girls Clubs of America

"Her book is a breezy read for such deep subject matter, but her beautiful and prevailing spirit shines through on every page."

—Pacific Northwest *Inlander*

"An engaging memoir of a dancing life."

—*The Philadelphia Inquirer*

"So well-written and . . . so forthcoming."

—BlackNews.com

"Captivating."

—*The Kansas City Star*

"Copeland's depiction of the drive that pushed her to succeed in a white-dominated art form is inspiring."

—*Kirkus Reviews*

"A tale of hardship and remarkable success."

—*Los Angeles Magazine*

"Instead of rags to riches, Copeland goes from baggy shorts to leotards as she navigates the whitewashed world of ballet."

—*Library Journal*

"The perfect inspiration."

—*Dance Teacher* magazine

"She embodies both fearlessness and femininity, reflecting the life of contradictions and obstacles over which she's leapt so beautifully. If ever a solo ballerina was poised to become a household name, it's now."

—Yahoo!

MISTY COPELAND

with Charisse Jones

Life in Motion

An Unlikely Ballerina

A Touchstone Book

Published by Simon & Schuster

New York   London   Toronto   Sydney   New Delhi

Touchstone
A Division of Simon & Schuster, Inc.
1230 Avenue of the Americas
New York, NY 10020

First Touchstone trade paperback edition December 2014

For information about special discounts for bulk purchases,
please contact Simon & Schuster Special Sales
at 1-866-506-1949 or business@simonandschuster.com.

The Simon & Schuster Speakers Bureau can bring authors to your live event.
For more information or to book an event contact
the Simon & Schuster Speakers Bureau
at 1-866-248-3049 or visit our website at www.simonspeakers.com.

Interior design by Ruth Lee-Mui
Jacket design by Marlyn Dantes
Jacket photograph by Gregg Delman

Manufactured in the United States of America

9   10   8

Library of Congress Cataloging-in-Publication data is available.

ISBN 978-1-4767-3798-0
ISBN 978-1-4767-3799-7 (pbk)
ISBN 978-1-4767-3800-0 (ebook)

Insert photos: p. 3, top: Rosalie O'Connor; p. 6: Getty Images; p. 7, top (inset):
Marcia E. Wilson; with Herman Cornejo: Gene Schiavone;
p. 8: Rosalie O'Connor. All other photos from the author's personal collection.

To all ballerinas and dancers of the world.
Our art is vital. Let's keep it alive, growing, and expanding!

Prologue

IT'S MORNING. EIGHT A.M., to be exact. My alarm goes off for no more than five seconds before I sit up to stop the nagging sound.

As I stretch my arms, I realize how achy my body is. Still, it's a wonderful aching every dancer knows.

As many busy New Yorkers do, I click a few buttons on my computer and order my morning coffee—black, no sugar—and blueberry muffin from the corner deli to be delivered to the door of my Upper West Side apartment. Class starts at ten thirty at the Met.

The ordinary rituals of my day belie what will be an extraordinary evening. I'm eager for this day to start so that, later, I can rise again, this time on the stage of the Metropolitan Opera House.

Tonight, I will become the first black woman to star in Igor Stravinsky's iconic role for American Ballet Theatre, one of the most prestigious dance companies in the world.

As the Firebird.

This is for the little brown girls.

My barre warm-up this morning would be familiar to any ballet dancer, whether she's an apprentice in Moscow or a seven-year-old taking his first ballet class in Detroit. It's slow structured yet fragmentary—perfectly designed to bring me to center, where I can dance freely without the barre, each motion a broken-down version of what tonight's solos will be. I start with *pliés*, increasingly deeper bends of the knee which warm up my legs while still allowing them the support that they need. I transition to larger movements of the leg, circling them in my *ronds de jambe*, and bending them in *fondus*, gradually stretching my hips and knees. I finish with a *port de bras*, stretching my torso forward and from side to side.

I move to center, where each aerobic exercise moves more fluidly to the next without the barre's strictures. I know that each graceful *glissade*—where I jump in first position with both legs flicking to a dagger before closing into fifth—stems from that disengaged brush of the leg where my foot leaves the floor, which stems from a *tendu*, a single pointed toe that I've extended while maintaining contact with the floor.

Ballets are just stylized versions of these seemingly basic movements on a grand scale. If the basic strength and elegance of a barre class is like slipping on a little black dress, the challenge of dancing a full three-act ballet is like learning to accessorize for any occasion. I have to think about whether I want to add sass or longing or, as I will tonight, the exotic, otherworldly energy of the mythical Firebird.

You have to know the appropriate way to adorn each story and character with your body. *Sleeping Beauty*, for example, is very elegant and regal; its movements are fluid, with few accents. There are certain ways you have to hold your torso, position your head, and use your arms as a certain character that can differ from what I rehearse in class. The difference between being an amazing technician and being a soloist or principal is mastering those interpretive flourishes to tell the best story. Otherwise you aren't a ballerina—you're just another dancer.

No matter how old you are or how long you've been dancing, ballet professionals know that we have to repeat these steps in class every day to maintain the strength and the clean positioning that's so essential to dancers. I'm constantly working on my technique. Even a single day off can cause my muscles to forget what my mind knows by heart. I take class seven days a week, even though the company only works five days each week.

I know that I'll never perfect the ballet technique—ever. That's why I love it so much. It never becomes boring, even though I've done all these movements in this very studio a million times over thirteen years. It's my safe place, where I can experiment. I sweat, grunt, and make faces that would never pass on the Metropolitan Opera House stage. It's the time to push myself beyond my limits so that my performances can feel effortless, fresh.

Not everyone wants to push themselves to that brink of breaking, but it's what you commit to when you're a professional—the very present reality that you may break instead of bend.

Today, I don't jump. My left shin has been hurting, and I don't want to risk straining it before tonight's performance.

I have always been known as a jumper, able to soar to great heights and land like a feather on the stage. The Firebird flutters and flies. But it has been difficult to practice her grand jumps the past several weeks. The pain in my leg has been intense, and I've had to save every bit of my strength for the actual performances.

By now, I am as familiar with the feral gestures of the Firebird as I am with my own breath, my own heartbeat. American Ballet Theatre's spring season has been under way for six weeks, with two more to go, and I've previously performed as the Firebird twice in Southern California, barely an hour away from my hometown.

I have a light rehearsal around noon at the Met, to space the choreography and get the feel of the stage. I want to be sure that I hit all of my marks, that I'm always in the right place so I don't collide with the corps de ballet during my variations or move out of sync with my partner when we dance our *pas de deux*.

When the public walks into the hallowed space of the Metropolitan Opera, it sees its gilded foyer, its luxe patron boxes, and its grand stage. But behind the scenes there are studio spaces where performers can hone their magic, eking out a final practice before the show begins.

I spend part of the afternoon in one of those rooms for a private rehearsal with Alexei Ratmansky, *Firebird*'s choreographer.

Alexei, ever the visionary and perfectionist, is changing the choreography up until the last minute. He tweaks a leap here, a twist there. We go through all my solos to ensure that the counts are exactly right.

Beat one. *On my toes.*

Beat two. *Dart to the right.*

Beat three. *Bound through the air.*

Alexei changes my entrance to the stage several times before we finally agree on the steps that best suit me. There are two other casts, and the Firebird's entrance in each is different, difficult, unique. I feel energized. I feel ready.

This is for the little brown girls.

I walk home to my apartment, a dozen blocks from the Met. I shower and flip to the Food Network just to have some background noise as I try to relax my mind, wind down my body.

A couple hours later, I'm back at the Met. The curtain won't go up until seven thirty p.m., and I won't take the stage until nine, but I want to be early, to not have to rush.

It is a special evening, and not just for me. Kevin McKenzie, ABT's artistic director, is also being honored. It is his twentieth anniversary in that role, and in celebration there will be speeches, a video tribute featuring congratulations from the artistic directors of nearly every major classical company in the world, and performances by all of ABT's principal dancers.

It's getting close to showtime. I have been a soloist for five years, and the eleven of us have a dressing room all to ourselves. But I have never used it. I prefer the comforting camaraderie of the dressing area shared by the *corps.* I spent six years as part of the corps de ballet, and with them I want to remain, preparing for my first principal role in a classical ballet surrounded by loving friends. Nothing feels different between us, even though I'll dance the lead. That, at least, provides normalcy on this extraordinary night.

I have my own corner of the dressing room, claimed long ago. The table is so crowded with flowers and chocolates and photographs that there is barely room for me to squeeze my cell phone. There are bouquets of orchids, my favorite, and dozens of roses. Arthur Mitchell, the founder of Dance Theatre of Harlem, has left me a voice mail, wishing me luck. There are dozens more e-mails, texts, and cards—from friends, family, and fans all over the country—wishing me well.

Looking at the beautiful bounty, I start to get emotional. But I can't be distracted. I can't be overwhelmed.

This is for the little brown girls.

I go into hair and makeup about a half hour after the evening performance starts. In the mirror, Misty disappears and a mystical creature takes her place, its face dusted with red glitter and painted with dazzling red spirals that shoot from the corners of its eyes. Even my inch-long false lashes are colored red. One of the company's dressers slicks back my hair into a smooth swirl to better attach my red and gold plume.

"Good luck, Misty," a dancer hollers at me with a smile.

"Merde!" one yells.

"Enjoy it!" says another.

I know that they wholeheartedly mean what they say. But those are everyday salutations that can be tossed out before any night's performance. They don't reflect the monumental nature of this evening, what it means to me and the rest of the African American community.

Maybe no words could.

Fifteen minutes.

I plop down on the floor of the dressing area's lounge, stretching, flexing, staring at myself in the mirror. I stamp that thought down as quickly as it emerges. I think to myself, *This is it, this is my moment.* Finally, the moment to shine, to prove myself, to represent black dancers at the highest level of ballet.

This is for the little brown girls.

But my shin is throbbing uncontrollably.

I know deep down that I can't go on much longer with such pain. Tonight will be the first time I perform as the Firebird in New York, and I pray it won't be my last. By the time *Firebird* is up, ABT has performed several other pieces and two intermissions have paused the program.

I make my way toward the stage. Kevin McKenzie, the conductor, and the rest of ABT's artistic staff are standing there, behind the curtain, wishing me luck.

I remember the first time I stood on the stage at the Metropolitan Opera House. I was nineteen years old, still struggling to find my place in ABT's corps de ballet. I traced the marley floor with my pointe shoes and imagined myself on the stage, not as a member of the corps, but as a principal dancer. It felt right. It felt like a promise: someday, somehow, it was going to happen for me.

A decade later, I am here, waiting for the moment when I will explode onto the stage in a burst of red and gold.

Outside, the largest crowd I have ever seen waits. Prominent members of the African American community and trailblazers in the world of dance who have seldom received their due are here tonight: Arthur Mitchell, Debra Lee, Star Jones, Nelson George . . . but I know I will also dance for those who aren't here, who have never seen a ballet, who pass the Metropolitan Opera House but cannot imagine what goes on inside. They may be poor, like I have been; insecure, like I have been; misunderstood, like I have been. I will be dancing for them, too. *Especially* for them.

This is for the little brown girls.

I stand in the farthest upstage wing when the curtain rises. There are a flock of "Firebirds" who enter the stage first after Ivan, the prince. I can feel the anticipation rolling off the crowd as they pose and preen. They expect me to be among them. I take a deep breath. The music starts, and with it comes the cheers, a great roar of love from the audience.

I realize in that moment that it doesn't matter what I do on the stage tonight. They are all here for me, *with me*, here for who I am and what tonight represents. I run onto the stage and feel myself transform. As I approach center, my flock parts, leaving me to stand alone. There's a brief second of silence before the audience erupts into applause once more, clapping so loudly I can barely hear the music.

And so it begins.

Chapter 1

∝

FROM THE TIME I turned two, my life was in constant motion.

That's how old I was when my mother loaded me, my sister, and my brothers onto a Greyhound bus in Kansas City and we left my father.

I was the youngest then, with lips and a nose like his, but I wouldn't know that for many years. I had no memories of him or photographs to remind me, and the next time I saw him, I would be twenty-two years old, traveling the world as a dancer with American Ballet Theatre, and Doug Copeland was just a middle-aged man whose temples had turned gray.

I was born in Kansas City, Missouri, my mother's second baby girl, and her fourth child. Two husbands later, our number would swell to six. When my mom squeezed our lives onto a bus headed west, our family began a pattern that would define my siblings' and my childhood: packing, scrambling, leaving—often barely surviving.

I don't remember the ride, but it took two days. Our final stop was the city of Bellflower, a working-class suburb of Los Angeles. We started anew there, and for a time that would turn out to be too brief, we had a home full of comfort and warmth, along with a new father.

His name was Harold. A childhood friend of my mother's, he met us at the bus station, and a little over a year later, he became her third husband. Harold was a sales executive for the Santa Fe Railroad, but his personality didn't match the stiffness of his title. He looked like the baseball player Darryl Strawberry in his home run–hitting prime—tall, muscular, and chestnut brown. Until my sister Lindsey was born three years later, I was the family's baby and tiny for my age. Harold would scoop me up in his strong arms and tickle me until I dissolved into tears of laughter.

Most of my earliest memories aren't of my mother, but of him. We kids were practically spilling out the front door and windows of our small apartment, but if our home sometimes resembled a three-ring circus, Harold was more the ringmaster than a parental figure committed to reining us in. He was a prankster with an infectious laugh. When my mother wanted him to discipline us kids, he would turn even that into a game.

"I'm not really going to spank you, but holler like I am," he'd whisper as he corralled us in the bedroom and shut the door. Then he'd take his broad palm and loudly slap the bed.

"No, Daddy, no," we'd scream, choking down giggles as we put on a performance we thought worthy of an Oscar. Mommy, satisfied and sitting in the living room, was none the wiser.

Despite there being so many of us, Harold would carve out

moments that made each of us feel like his only child. I remember loving sunflower seeds so much that my sisters and brothers took to calling me Bird. I trace my obsession to the times I would sit with Harold on the couch, the two of us alone together, popping seeds in our mouths and cracking the salty shells. Mommy hated it because the shells would fall between the cushions, making a mess. But memories of those afternoons remain precious to me.

That was the side of Harold we kids saw: cheerful, comforting, kind. But behind that facade of laughter and fun, my mother saw something entirely different. Harold was an alcoholic. We caught only glimpses of it, out the corners of our eyes, like the ever-present beer can on my parents' nightstand. But I later found out that what was mostly invisible to us was in Mommy's plain sight.

When I was eight or nine and we had a new home and a new daddy, Mommy would tell us stories of Harold not being in his right mind because of liquor, and how it sometimes frightened her.

When I was in middle school, Lindsey, his biological daughter, would often stay with him, and I would join them a few nights a week. By then, I had a best friend, Jackie Phillips. We were inseparable. I thought she was beautiful—lean with dark brown skin, she towered over me. We had most of our school activities in common.

Jackie lived right around the corner from our middle school, so Mommy didn't mind me staying there a couple of nights a week before Harold would come back to pick me up.

One night, Jackie and I were cracking up, blasting TLC's *CrazySexyCool* while we did our homework. The phone rang.

Jackie's mom yelled that it was for me. Lindsey was on the line, crying.

"Daddy's drunk," she said through her tears. "I told him that he shouldn't drive. Can you find another way home?"

I hung up the phone feeling sick to my stomach, not sure whether to tell Jackie's mother what was going on or to call Mommy.

I went back into Jackie's room. Time ticked by as I tried to figure out what to do. Too much time, as it turned out. The doorbell rang. It was Lindsey. Harold was waiting in the car.

I guess he knew better than to come to the door in his condition in front of Mrs. Phillips. When I got to the car, it reeked of cigarette smoke and beer. Harold put the key in the ignition and his foot on the gas, and we sped off over the Long Beach Bridge. My heart was pounding as the streetlights streaked by.

Lindsey and I sat in the backseat holding each other's hands tightly. This was truly the first time we understood the condition Mommy spoke of so often. We wove in and out of the lanes on the bridge that night at high speed, so close to the side rails hundreds of feet above the ocean. We feared for our lives. Yet there was something inside me and Lindsey that had such a strong image of Harold's warmth and gentleness that we did our best to never show him that we knew he was drunk or that it changed our perception of him.

The next time Lindsey called to tell me Harold was drunk, I asked to speak to him and told him that I would just spend the night at Jackie's, that he didn't have to pick me up.

I never loved Harold any less. To me, he remains one of the best parts of my childhood, the daddy who'd cook Lindsey and me waffles and serve them to us on plastic trays while we watched cartoons in our pajamas on Saturday mornings. I remember him sitting in the bathroom with me when I was four, holding my hand while I cried, straining from a stomachache. Memories of Harold are never cloudy, only clear and bright. And he's now been in recovery for fifteen years.

But five years after we'd arrived at Harold's apartment, Mommy decided that, once again, it was time to pick up and go.

Mommy strapped Lindsey into her car seat in the blue Mercedes station wagon while the rest of us squeezed in around her, finding space wherever we could. As we drove to God knew where, there was no tussling, no yelling. We were too confused to laugh, too scared to play around.

Our leaving was always like that—dramatic, hurried, and ragged.

Slender, not quite five feet six, until Mommy reached middle age she looked more like somebody's cool and sultry big sister than a mother of six. Mommy had long since retired her Kansas City Chiefs pom-poms, but she carried a cheerleader's exuberance throughout her life, rooting for her children and always smiling, despite too many marriages gone wrong and, at times, bill collectors on our trail.

To this day, I'm still trying to understand Mommy, all that shaped her and, most of all, the choices she made. She didn't talk much about her childhood, but from what I could glean, it was filled with pain. She was born to an Italian mother and an African American father, parents whom she would never know. They put her up for adoption, and while they didn't leave an explanation saying why they didn't keep her, I'm sure that, at a time when blacks and whites could go to jail for being married in many states, they peered into the future and figured that raising a biracial child was more than they could handle.

Mommy was given a home by an older African American couple, a social worker and her husband, but they died while she was still very young. From there she began to shuttle between the homes of various relatives and ended up mostly raising herself.

Leaving Harold was the beginning of a time when I could measure my days through my mother's boyfriends, her dependence on an ever-changing string of men. But all that clarity came later, when I was much older. On the night we left Harold, I was only seven, and the movements of my life weren't yet up to me. Our family was headed to San Pedro, a portside community nestled next to Los Angeles Harbor, and it would be the place to which we would always return, the place that, in between the picking up and leaving, my siblings and I would forever think of as home.

∝

I DON'T KNOW IF Harold knew that his wife and children were leaving him. But the man who eventually became our new stepfather knew that we were on our way. Robert, my mother's soon-to-be fourth husband, was the polar opposite of the man who had been her third. A successful radiologist, Robert was a little chubby, and, like my half-Italian, half-black mother, of mixed race, with bloodlines that were Hawaiian, Korean, Filipino, Portuguese, and Japanese.

A century earlier, fishermen from Japan, as well as from Croatia, Greece, and Italy, had plied San Pedro's waters for

sardines and albacore, making Los Angeles Harbor the biggest
fishing port in the country by the 1920s. Fishing was a hard
trade. Growing up, I heard of longshoremen who were killed on
the docks. But it was also a good living, and many of the local
men—my schoolmates' fathers, brothers, and uncles—chose to
answer the sea's call.

Life in San Pedro was etched by the sea, so much so that
I don't ever recall learning to swim, only that from the beginning of my time there I was able to glide through the water
effortlessly. When I hit my teens, my clothes would carry the
scent of burned wood from bonfires on the beach. And there
was many a school field trip to the Angel's Gate Lighthouse,
a structure built in 1913 that still serves as the port's sentry.
When a ship needs guidance, the foghorn pierces the quiet with
two blasts every thirty seconds. As a child, the sound must have
interrupted our games of jump rope, our lessons, our prayers.
But it blared so often that the longer we lived there, the less we
noticed it, and it faded into the background, like a heartbeat.

We were a part of Los Angeles but about as far from Hollywood, the city's flashy, mythical core, as you could get. Except
for the palm trees, San Pedro was a lot like Mayberry, the ficti-
tious country town that existed only on black-and-white TVs.
Generations lived and died there, unwilling to pull up the roots
that their grandparents had buried deep in the sandy soil.

There were no skyscrapers. Instead, downtown was like
a daguerreotype come to life, with gaslights and Victorian
shops. In San Pedro, it was the simple and familiar that mattered. Most of my old neighbors have no recollection of the
time I won a life-changing award dancing the role of Kitri in
Don Quixote at the Dorothy Chandler Pavilion, even though

my picture was splashed on the front of the *Daily Breeze*. But everyone still talks about the talent show at Point Fermin Elementary when I wore a white wedding dress and little, skinny Aaron, my classmate, serenaded me from down on his knees. That's the kind of thing that they remember in San Pedro: Aaron, my frilly costume, and a heartfelt but painfully off-key love song.

There were so many hills and curves on the way to Robert's home that it looked as if we would drive right into the Pacific Ocean before the car suddenly, mercifully, swerved and hugged the next bend. The house was a single story built in the Mediterranean style, with a huge front yard.

It was a perfect house on a perfect block—and what seemed like the portal to a perfect life. You could even see Catalina Island from the front porch, gleaming like a mirage in the morning fog. But what looks perfect is often just an illusion, like the dancer with a strained hamstring who wears a smile instead of a grimace when she lands as delicately as a butterfly despite her pain.

We kids didn't pay much attention to the beauty around us. We were too busy trying to figure out why we were here, what had gone wrong, and, most of all, when we would see Harold again. But this was home now, and soon we fell into the rhythms of our new life.

We had chores for the first time: taking out the garbage, washing the dishes, sweeping the breakfast crumbs off the floor. And there was no more grabbing a plate and eating on the couch. We sat down at the dining room table for our meals— morning, noon, and night.

That was okay. We Copelands were like a nomadic tribe:

hardy, fiercely protective of our band, and adaptable. We clung tightly to one another. And there were so many of us, we made our own party, our own fun, wherever we ended up and whatever the rules or circumstances.

My oldest sister, Erica, was twelve when we moved in with Robert. She was the most like our mother, vivacious and outspoken. She led our brood on the daily walks to school and tended to my bushel of hair, pulling it back into tight ponytails or blow-drying it straight after my bath.

Doug Jr., our oldest brother, was eleven, the namesake and, we would one day learn, the spitting image of our father. He was fiercely intelligent and so intent on gathering knowledge that he would curl up in the chair and read the dictionary the way other boys burrowed into comic books.

Like so many African Americans, our family was of mixed ancestry. We had an Italian grandmother on our mother's side, and our father was the son of a German woman and an African American man. But Doug Jr. stood firm in his blackness.

One day, when I was in third grade, I came home and found Doug Jr. sitting on the porch. His brow was furrowed as he fiddled with something small and white that he held in his hands.

"What are you doing?" I asked him.

"I'm reading about our history—about slavery—and I wanted to know what it felt like for our ancestors," he said. "So I'm picking cotton."

Unlike sand or seashells, raw cotton wasn't easy to find in San Pedro. But somehow he'd gotten ahold of some and was spending time picking the seeds out of a white wisp. That was quintessentially Doug: intense, conscious, and culturally curious.

After him came our brother Chris, who gave glimpses of the attorney he'd be one day in the way he'd argue every point with absolute conviction. If he was wrong, you'd better not tell him. He was fearless, playing every sport—tennis, basketball, football—at some point in our childhoods. He was so full of energy that he would sometimes just race around the house, literally crashing into the walls.

Our little sister Lindsey, who eventually sprinted her way to a track scholarship at Chico State University, was the baby born to Harold and my mother. She had a luminous smile and a raucous sense of humor like her father. And our baby brother Cameron, who would cry his way through T-ball but found his gift sitting in front of a piano, was born after our mother got involved with Robert.

Then there was me in the middle—quiet, introverted, and happy to disappear within the clamor of our rambunctious family.

I was a nervous child. And my unease, coupled with a perpetual quest for perfection, made my life much harder than it needed to be.

I think I was born worried. There wasn't a day that I didn't feel some kind of anxiety, especially in school, and my panic would begin from the moment I woke up, fretting that I would be late to homeroom, until I came back home in the early evening. I was just nervous about life, period. I felt awkward, as if I didn't fit in anywhere, and I lived in constant fear of letting my mother down, or my teachers, or myself.

It wasn't like Mommy was a scold. But you had to earn her praise, and I craved it desperately. With so many brothers and sisters, it was hard to command her attention, and my voice, muted by my intense shyness, could barely be heard above my siblings'.

I strived to be perfect at school as well. The thought of being tardy could set my heart to racing. The summer before I was to follow Erica, Doug, and Chris to Dana Middle School, I constantly reminded myself that Mommy and I had to pay it a visit so I could memorize every turn and twist: which staircase led to algebra, where my English class was in the building. I was terrified of getting lost and then having to walk in front of a sea of staring faces when I arrived after the bell.

Mommy refused to accommodate my summertime walk-through. She was always trying to get me to relax, to calm down. But later, when I was in high school and could make the trek on my own, no one could deter me from my pre–Labor Day route rehearsal or the other strategies I devised to avoid being late. Pretty much all the way through twelfth grade, I would get to school an hour early, plant myself on the floor in front of my locker, and study until it was time to go to my first class.

I was never late, not even once.

❧

I REMEMBER WHEN I appeared onstage for the first time. I was five years old, but unlike my later performances, what I most recall is not the confidence I felt in front of the crowd, or the rush from the applause, but the way Mommy reacted after the show.

We were still living in Bellflower with Harold, and Mommy entered Chris, Erica, and me into the talent show at Thomas Jefferson Elementary School.

She made our costumes, and we practiced for weeks, shaking our hips and lip-synching to "Please Mr. Postman." I caught on quickly and I loved the experience, running home every day after school, practicing in the living room. Most of all, it was fun to see my mother so excited, especially when she was getting us ready the night of the performance.

"Oh yes, wait a minute, Mister Postman."

It was showtime. Erica and I channeled the Marvelettes, while Chris, seven years old and dressed in navy blue shorts and a white shirt, toted a satchel and tossed envelopes to the audience. We were a hit, especially with Mommy.

"You guys were great!" she gushed afterward, snapping our pictures and beaming as members of the audience came over to tell us how cute we were. "You are naturals! Misty, you belong on the stage."

I felt so special that night. Even though I'd shared the spotlight with Erica and Chris, I felt for once that I'd stood out from the crowd of little Copelands, that Mommy's attention was focused solely on me.

That happened only occasionally, like when I got a good report card or was picked to be a hall monitor at Dana Middle School. Mommy would bring me bags of sunflower seeds as a treat, or stationery with sketches of sunflowers, or a sickly sweet kiddie perfume called—what else—Sunflower. I would gleefully accept my rewards, clinging to Mommy's attention for as long as I could.

I didn't feel particularly good at anything when it came to school. So instead I worked incredibly hard, going over equations, pronouns, and dates of Civil War battles until they were imprinted on my brain. I aced pretty much every exam, but it would not be until I found ballet in my teenage years that I would realize the true gift of my visual memory—the ability to see movement and quickly imitate it.

My first model for movement wasn't a dancer at all. It was a gymnast, Nadia Comaneci. I wasn't born when Comaneci made history in the 1976 Olympics, becoming the first woman to score a perfect 10 in gymnastics and winning gold medals for her strength and elegance on the balance beam and parallel bars. Instead, I discovered her when I was seven and saw her story depicted in a Lifetime movie. Smitten, I recorded the broadcast on our VCR and would sit on the floor in front of the TV, pressing the rewind button so I could watch it again and again. I became obsessed with gymnastics, tuning in to any meet or exhibition that I could find. But from the start, I was more drawn to the floor exercises than the aerial acrobatics—probably, I realize now, because it was the closest thing to classical movement and dance that I'd ever seen.

I started to teach myself gymnastics, and my body knew what my mind didn't yet comprehend: that rhythmic motion came as naturally to me as breathing. In our new home with Robert, we had huge yards in front and back, and I would stretch out barefoot on the grass, teaching myself how to do backbend walkovers, cartwheels, handstands. I already knew how to do the splits, though no one had ever shown me. My legs just slid into position. I could balance on my head the way others stood firmly on their feet. I didn't question why I could instantly do moves that it might take others months to achieve, why my arms and legs had the elasticity of a rubber band. They just did, and I just knew.

I spent hours after school and on weekends practicing my

backyard routines. Then when I was done, I would arch my back, throw up my arms, and let the applause only I could hear wash over me. Just like Nadia.

Eventually, I realized that I didn't really want to be a gymnast. It was the floor routines that transfixed me, not all the tumbling and flips. But for the first time, I'd tapped into the power of movement and felt its meditative grace. In it, I'd found an escape.

IT WAS AROUND THIS time that I began to get my first migraine headaches. Mommy told me that she had started getting them at around the same age. It was genetic, but I think that the crippling pain I experienced, as well as the vomiting and blurred vision, came mainly from stress. I was a constant ball of fear.

I would leave school early some days, too sick to study or play, falling asleep in my clothes as soon as I reached my bed. Light exacerbated my pain, so I had to lie in a pitch-black room. Robert would wake me when he got home from work and help me change into my pajamas. Over the years, my pain became routine but no less severe.

There was never a moment's quiet in my house. There was a person sprawled on every chair, a book or toy tossed in every corner. We woke up every morning to a wall of sound, with children yelling, music blaring, and the television on full blast.

The TV became our family altar because that was how we watched sports. It didn't matter which sport, what game, or which team: the Chicago Bulls, the San Francisco 49ers. Everyone had his or her favorite—everyone, that is, except me. But the Kansas City Chiefs belonged to us all. Before we children were born, my mother had become a Kansas City Chiefs cheerleader just so she could get free tickets to see the team play.

On house-shaking, popcorn-spilling weekends and Monday nights, the rest of the family would gather in the living room and roar over every stolen yard and fumbled pass. My mom and my siblings were consumed by it. I, on the other hand, would retreat to a bedroom, crank up a pop aria by Mariah Carey, and create. I didn't know it was called choreographing at the time.

It was more hip swaying and head bopping than anything else. Mirroring the dancing I saw in the music videos that were constantly on the TV, I'd perform a pantomime, literally acting out a song's lyrics.

"I've been THINKING about YOU," Mariah would sing. I'd point my fingers at my temples, and then stretch my arms out to my imaginary boyfriend, hips and shoulders pumping to the beat.

Then she crooned that she was falling in love. I'd flutter my arms and slowly drop to the floor.

No, it wasn't exactly George Balanchine. But I could easily imagine myself directing a video for MTV.

Sometimes I would pull Lindsey into my game so I could see my creation brought to life by another body. She was an unwilling student to say the least, probably because of all of us kids, Lindsey had inherited zero rhythm. We used to tease her mercilessly, asking if she'd been dropped into the wrong family or was secretly a white girl in cocoa skin.

"Please, Lindsey, do this dance for me," I'd beg.

"I don't wannnoooo," she'd wail, tears welling in her eyes.

"I'll get Chris and Doug to give up the TV and let you watch *Sister, Sister*," I'd cajole.

That's usually all it took. Lindsey loved her some Tia and Tamera Mowry. But she'd pout her way through every step.

Though I discovered dance while we lived with Robert, its true role as my sanctuary was yet to develop. Ours was a chaotic life. We had a house and interludes of stability when my mother had a husband, and crowded, cluttered apartments when we lived life in between.

"Ooh, child, things are gonna get easier. / Ooh, child, things are gonna get brighter." I'd sashay around Mommy's bedroom, listening to Tupac, hoping he was right.

"Bam." I'd fan my hands in front of my face, and swing my hips to the left, rocking out to Salt-N-Pepa's "Whatta Man."

"Pop." I'd jerk my head to the right, my arms undulating while Craig Mack gave me "Flava in Ya Ear."

When I was a girl, I loved watching reruns of *The Brady Bunch*. The six kids shared rooms in their spotless house, and the biggest crises they ever faced was Marcia's skin breaking out the night before the senior prom or Greg's voice changing on the eve of a talent show.

When we eventually left Robert, like we had Harold and my father before him, and our family had to give up our blue station wagon, I would ride the bus and daydream about all the things a little girl should have that I didn't: a mommy who cooked dinner for her family; a big, sparkling clean house; and problems no bigger than a pimple.

But whenever I danced, whenever I created, my mind was clear. I didn't think about how I slept on the floor because I didn't have a bed, when my mother's new boyfriend might become my next stepfather, or if we would be able to dig up enough quarters to buy food. My worries would dissolve with the dance, and there was no crisis that a Mariah Carey song couldn't cure.

My love of performing was an unlikely one. At school, I was still so afraid of being called on in class that my stomach would tremble.

"Misty," Mrs. Schweble, our sixth-grade English teacher, would bellow from the front of the room. "Please read the next sentence."

I'd shakily clutch my copy of *The Catcher in the Rye.*

"'Life is a game, boy,'" I read, my words catching in my throat before rushing out in a breathless squeak. "'Life is a game that one plays according to the rules.'"

But for a little girl who lived in terror of making a mistake, of being embarrassed or criticized in front of others, the stage was somehow an oasis. I came to understand why when I later became a part of ABT, performing at the Metropolitan Opera in New York, the Bolshoi Theatre in Moscow, the Bunka Kaikan in Tokyo.

As a professional, you have to endure a tremendous amount of criticism and judgment leading up to a performance. You can barely take a step in rehearsal before the dance mistress will clap, stop you, and give you a critique.

But during the actual performance, when the music swells, and the crowd hushes, it's all up to you—how high you leap, when you breathe. There's no more time to worry or try to make it better. It either works or it doesn't. You land with grace or you stumble and fall. That absoluteness, that finality, is freedom. And the stage was the one place where I felt it.

I knew all that even as a child. Only then, the stage wasn't buffering me from the ballet mistress or dance critics. Instead, it allowed me to forget my worries about not fitting in, my embarrassment about Mommy's being married so many times, the ache I felt on the days when I couldn't see Harold.

When I was in the sixth grade, I decided that I would choreograph a dance for my two best friends, Danielle and Reina, and me to perform in the annual Point Fermin Elementary School talent show. Danielle, part Mexican American and part white, with long dark brown hair, towered over our troika. Reina, a mixture of Mexican American and Asian ancestry, was tiny and brown, like me. We three were inseparable. I would go over to Danielle's house every afternoon after school, and we'd hang out, doing our homework and dancing to New Edition and Boyz II Men. We were sisters, Danielle and Reina and me.

But I didn't let my affection get in the way of cracking the whip hard during the mandatory rehearsals that I called leading up to the show. We would line up in Danielle's living room, me in front, and practice our routine. Unfortunately, Danielle and Reina lacked my passion, and on the Friday night when we finally hit the talent show stage, their less-than-enthusiastic preparation was glaringly revealed in the auditorium's hazy white lights.

As I lip-synched to Mariah Carey's "I've Been Thinking About You," Reina and Danielle danced awkwardly behind me, mixing up their steps. Disappointment doesn't begin to describe how I felt. But I didn't doubt the excellence of my own performance for a moment. Out there, in front of the crowd, under the pinpoint of my elementary school's spotlight, I felt fierce.

The next time I performed like that, it was the following

school year, and I was the new kid at Dana Middle School, trying to follow Erica's lead and win a place on the school's drill team.

Dana's drill team was legendary. It swept the competitions held throughout the state, and my sister Erica had been one of its stars. She had always been my idol: beautiful, popular, and never seeming to suffer even for a moment the self-doubt that often paralyzed me. I wanted to be just like her. And because the trepidation that dogged every other part of my life seemed to disappear when it came to the thought of performing, I wasn't aiming just to be part of the team: I wanted to be captain.

Trying out for captain meant I needed to perform two routines: one that all prospective members of the drill team would have to dance, and an individual routine that I would create and perform on my own. Erica agreed to help me with the choreography but warned that the drill team would likely not be the same storied group it had been when she was part of it. The coach who had guided it to so many wins had left the school at the end of the previous school year and a recently hired history teacher, Elizabeth Cantine, was taking her place.

I still wanted to try out. Our family loved George Michael, post-Wham, and we decided I would dance to "I Want Your Sex." Erica and I practiced every day after school.

But Erica wasn't happy with my performance. It seems that I wasn't properly carrying out her creative vision. Eventually, she erupted in frustration.

"You can't remember anything!" she screamed one afternoon, before she stormed out of the living room, leaving me in tears. It was a curious critique, given that, years later, choreographers would specifically seek to work with me because of my gift of recalling and mimicking their steps instinctively. But that day, if it had been up to Erica, I wouldn't have been cast in a low-budget music video, let alone a performance of *Le Corsaire.*

I begged her to come back and help, but Erica refused, so I finished working out the routine on my own. Two days later, I showed up for tryouts in the school gym. It was my first audition—the first of what would become a lifetime of proving my skills.

I felt a little intimidated standing before the judging table. Behind it were three school-yard prima donnas who seemed to relish the chance to dish out a bit of what they'd gotten the year before when they'd been the nervous neophytes trying to grab spots on the team. Next to them sat the new coach, Elizabeth. She was birdlike and tiny, like me, with brown curls framing her calm gaze, and her features were as delicate as bone china.

I danced with the dozens of other girls trying out for the team. Then it was time for my solo.

I stood straight, eyes to the ground, hands folded, one knee poked out, waiting for the tape to start.

"*Baaaaby,*" George Michael shouted, and I was off. I stomped, spun, and gyrated my hips for the next three minutes, ending the routine by sliding into a split, my arm stretched out in front of me, eyes fixed on the ceiling.

Silence.

"Thank you," an auburn-haired drill-team diva said curtly, making notes on a yellow legal pad.

But I caught Elizabeth smiling.

Back home that evening, I paced around the living room,

butterflies skittering in my stomach, waiting to find out if I'd been chosen. The phone rang.

Not only had I made the team, I'd been named captain.

Now my days had a new ripple. Drill-team practice was during my sixth-period PE class, which was a good thing because my school day was packed. I was sixth-grade treasurer and also a commodore, Dana Middle School's fancy name for a hall monitor.

The thirty of us girls who made up the drill squad would gather in a room adjacent to our school gym. We'd wear our gym clothes to practice but put on our school colors for the games, teeny yellow skirts with blue-and-white trim that we made even shorter by rolling them up. We had yellow V-neck tops with thick straps, and white rubber-soled slip-on shoes that resembled Keds. My shirt had CAPTAIN MISTY in the corner, embroidered in white thread.

Being drill-team captain made me automatically popular, but I didn't really feel I fit in with the others on the team. Some of the girls were older than me since my September birthday meant I was among the youngest in my grade. And I was a nerd, still playing with Barbies and having nightmares about showing up for Spanish class unprepared for my oral exam because I'd somehow forgotten that it was finals week.

My drill teammates, on the other hand, were what Mommy called "fast," slathering on pink and purplish lip gloss and rimming their eyes with black eyeliner. While I was carrying out my duties as hall monitor, making sure everyone was getting to class on time, they were leaning against their lockers talking about who they wanted to make out with on the basketball team.

I never really hung out with those girls outside of practice or games. My best friend was still Jackie, who, like me, was in student government. We'd sit together at lunch and have sleepovers at her house on weekends.

But my teammates were friendly enough, and more than that, they showed me respect. There was no question that I danced the best and that's why *I* was captain. When I was in that practice room, I found my voice.

It wasn't called drill team for nothing.

"Aten-hut!" I'd yell. *"Left face!"*

I was the littlest thing on the team, but the girls listened attentively and did whatever I commanded. I loved that power, but the confidence it brought would disappear and my anxiety would return as soon as practice was over and I went back to a life where I was terrified of losing my footing and crashing down.

There was one other space, however, where I felt at least somewhat comfortable—the San Pedro Boys and Girls Club. Every day after school, I'd walk the two blocks there and hang out with my siblings until Mommy got off work and came to take us home.

DRILL-TEAM PRACTICE WAS NOT what I'd expected. Elizabeth had been trained in classical ballet as a child, and she incorporated some of its basic technique into warm-ups and choreography. The first day we all got together, I stood on tiptoe as Elizabeth instructed, stepped to my right with arms open, and closed them, spinning around. *Chaîné*, the name of the step, was unfamiliar to me, but the *whoosh* of momentum when I spun was like the surge I felt when I did a cartwheel in our yard.

Elizabeth taught me to bend my knees, twirl, and quickly shift my weight to one leg, bringing the other up into a bent angle, before landing on my toes. She called that a *piqué*. I thought the names of the steps were unusual, but the movements themselves never felt foreign to me.

A few weeks into the school year, I got the idea of choreographing a routine for the drill team to Mariah Carey's "All I Want for Christmas Is You." It became my obsession. I even put the sewing skills I'd learned from Robert's mother, Grandma Marie, to good use, making all the costumes myself.

I asked Elizabeth to use some of the drill-team budget to buy us red leotards and I spent a couple weeks sewing little red skirts with fake fur trim. I loved doing things like that: sewing, crafting, imagining, creating. I retrieved red canes, left in the school basement from a long-ago Christmas show, and wrapped them with white tape for us to use as props onstage.

I was determined that the team would have the steps down cold—there would be no repeat of the disastrous talent show with Reina and Danielle. I even ordered rehearsals on the weekends to make sure the performance would be perfect. There were *piqués*, and leaps, and *pirouettes* with the girls' knees facing forward—like jazz choreography, I later realized—instead of the perfectly aligned turnout that Elizabeth would sometimes have us practice.

It was a mélange of all the new steps that the team had learned from Elizabeth. But for our finale, we used a move as familiar as "Jingle Bells," lining up like the Radio City Rockettes, kicking our heels high in the air.

The audience gave us a standing ovation.

Our Christmas show came at the end of the semester, and then we were off for the two-week winter break. When we came back, Elizabeth said she wanted to talk with me.

"You know, you have the perfect physique for ballet and a natural ability," she said. "I know you go to the Boys and Girls Club after school. A friend of mine teaches a ballet class there. Her name is Cindy Bradley. Why don't you check it out?"

I was caught off guard. Ballet? Why would I want to do that?

I had never even seen one. I can't remember if I had much of an impression of what one might be like—maybe lyrical and slow like the dance Elizabeth had the drill team do once with giant ribbons?

I'd enjoyed that since all movement was fun for me. But what I found frightening was the thought of going beyond my comfort zone. I didn't know the ballet teacher at the Boys and Girls Club, and the idea of seeking out this stranger to start learning a dance form I knew nothing about intimidated me.

Still, that afternoon, because my coach had asked me to and I always did what I was told, I dutifully walked to the Boys and Girls Club gym, crept quietly into the bleachers, and sat with my arms wrapped around my knees, watching. For the next week or so, I was an audience of one for a dozen or so girls and a couple of boys, most of whom were younger than me, pointing, tapping, bending, and stretching. One day, their teacher, Cindy, glanced back and walked over.

"I've seen you sitting here every day. What are you doing?" she asked me.

"My drill-team coach, Elizabeth Cantine, told me to come check it out," I said quietly. "She thinks I'd be good at it."

"She told me about you," Cindy said, her eyes widening with recognition. "Why don't you come join us?"

But I couldn't bring myself to. Not yet. The other girls clearly had been at it for a while. And they also looked the part, with their smooth slippers, crisp pink tights, and colorful leotards. How would I fit in?

"I don't have a leotard or tights," I mumbled.

"Don't worry about that," Cindy said. "Just wear your gym clothes."

Another week passed with me sitting and watching. I didn't tell my brothers and sisters I was going to the gym because I didn't want them to try to convince me to try something I was scared to do. What if I took the class and made a fool of myself? What would go through the other kids' minds? What would Elizabeth think when Cindy reported back to her?

"She couldn't follow a single thing I said," I imagined Cindy saying, shaking her head, still stunned by how pitiful I was. "This girl needs to stick to the drill team."

Finally, one afternoon I told myself that if I was going to go to the gym at the Boys and Girls Club anyway, I might as well give it a try. I went into the locker room to change and emerged, slightly embarrassed, in blue cotton shorts long enough to scrape my knees, my white T-shirt, and a pair of old gym socks. I willed myself to walk to the center of the basketball court.

I found a place. I stood up tall, gazed straight ahead, and, for the first time, lay my hand on the barre.

❧

Chapter 2

I QUIT.

That's what I muttered to myself as I walked out of that first class at the Boys and Girls Club, determined that it would also be my last. I'd spent an hour feeling like a broken marionette, twisting my torso, stretching my arms, uncertain all the while of what I was doing.

Was this even dance? Standing in a line with a dozen girls, spending an hour practicing how to flex your toes, hold your arms, bend your knees? This wasn't anything like the stomps and jumps I loved on the drill team.

I scurried past the gym on my way to other activities the next day, the day after, and the day after that. But Cindy wasn't giving up. About a week after I'd decided I had no interest in continuing, she spotted me.

"Misty!" she called, "can you come here for a second?"

Trapped, I reluctantly followed her to the front of her class. This was about as bad as it could get for nervous old me. I'd felt overwhelmed in that first class; it was too much information coming too fast, and I was way behind the other students. I hated feeling unprepared and confused. And now to have all eyes fixed on me when I didn't know what I was doing? I was scared to death.

But Cindy proceeded to gently stretch and mold my body into various positions, using me as an example for the other kids. She lifted my leg to my ear, tugged and flexed my feet. Whatever pose she conjured, I was able to hold. Cindy said that in all her years of dancing, in all her years of teaching, she had never seen anyone quite like me.

I'm not sure I believed her. But her praise piqued my curiosity, and I sheepishly joined the rest of the students at the barre, deciding to give her classes another try.

Cynthia Bradley could be very persuasive.

You knew she was a free spirit from the first time you met her. She wore her flaming red hair in a short, sleek bob; and her big, glittering earrings were so heavy they pulled at her lobes. It almost made me wonder how her thin, long frame didn't topple over from their weight.

She would tell me later that from the time she was a little girl and heard "King of the Road" on her parents' record player, she knew that she wanted to be onstage, singing and dancing in front of an audience much larger than the family members who watched her sing along with Roger Miller in the living room. She studied ballet as a child and got a chance to dance professionally when she was seventeen, performing with the Virginia Ballet Company and Louisville Ballet, among others. But she suffered an injury soon after and had to give up her career before it really had the chance to blossom.

So she switched from dance to music. She renamed herself "Cindy Vodo" and started a punk band called the Wigs that became a little bit of a big deal in the San Pedro punk scene. They had hits like "Stiff Me" that got a lot of radio play in the 1980s. But Cindy still relied on ballet to pay the rent. She started a school in Palos Verdes, an upscale pocket of Southern California not far from San Pedro, so she could teach ballet on the side. She eventually even married one of her dance students, Patrick Bradley, who, I would later learn, was as steady and serene as Cindy was flighty and dramatic.

The Wigs wound up settling in San Pedro because it was close to the heart of the L.A. music business, and also near Laguna Niguel, where most of the members worked their day jobs. Cindy, likewise, moved her teaching there, starting the San Pedro Ballet School with Patrick.

Cindy straddled the lines between elegance and eccentricity, self-absorption and altruism. But Cindy would also make me—a girl with knees that curved backward even when I stood straight, my size 7 feet that were still too large for my stick-figure frame—feel like the most beautiful and loved little ballerina in the world. I'd never met anyone like her.

Those first afternoons in her class at the Boys and Girls Club, I would walk from school and take my place among a dozen or so other budding dancers. They stretched and bowed, their brows creased in concentration. But Cindy, staring attentively, seemed to focus solely on me.

The class was very basic. We learned only the most fundamental steps of ballet.

First position: heels together, toes pointed in opposite directions.

Second position: the same, but with space wide enough to slip two feet between your heels.

Third position: the heel of one foot meeting the arch of the other.

Fourth position: one foot turned out in front of the other, with about a foot of space in between.

Fifth position: your feet turned out but crossed in front of each other, parallel like an equal sign.

Ballet teachers usually create combinations, mixing and matching the steps and positions of ballet technique for their students to execute, but Cindy kept it simple.

She would lead, and I tentatively strayed from the barre to follow. I stood on my tiptoes and held out my arms as though I was cradling a giant balloon. My arms were rounded, floating, strong enough not to drop my imaginary sphere but soft enough not to make it pop. Then I spun around, lifting one foot and placing it down into fifth position, again and again until I had made my way halfway across the gym—my first *pirouettes.*

One afternoon, I lifted my arms above my head and leaped, my right leg stretched straight in front, my left leg extended backward. It was like the splits I would do in the backyard or during drill-team practice, only in the air. My first *grand jeté.*

I would do many more. And in those moments, when I was soaring, getting stronger, going higher, I felt exhilarated.

Cindy was impressed, whatever I did.

"It's just amazing that you can already do all these things," she'd murmur, after I'd done an *arabesque* or she'd bent me this way and that.

My body yielded to her every suggestion. It was as if I'd been doing ballet all my life, and my limbs instinctively remembered what my conscious mind had somehow forgotten. I didn't question it, but I didn't take it for granted, either. Just like with my schoolwork, my drill-team choreography, and anything else I set out to do, my overwhelming need to please—to be perfect—was there in ballet class, too.

So were my insecurities. Despite my prowess, ballet class still felt like being thrown into the deep end of the pool when I'd only just become brave enough to stick my face in the water. Walking into the gym each day, I continued to feel like an outsider. Instead of the leotard and tights that were de rigueur, I was still wearing the baggy clothes I put on for drill-team practice each day. And as I looked at my dance mates, it became clear that, by ballet standards, I was ancient.

Most ballerinas start to dance when they are sipping juice boxes in preschool. I was thirteen years old. Self-doubt taunted me.

"You're too old. You're behind. You'll never catch up."

But Cindy disagreed. She'd found what she was looking for.

Cindy's stint at the Boys and Girls Club was always meant to be temporary. Her studio, the San Pedro Dance Center, was in another corner of the community that was far more affluent and much less diverse than mine. But her desire to share the magic and discipline of dance with those who otherwise might not be exposed to it brought her to South Cabrillo Avenue. She and Mike Lansing, the head of our Boys and Girls Club, were friends, and together they had the idea of turning the club into a sort of feeder program, or scouting base.

She'd come to teach the basics of ballet to underprivileged children, then pick out those who were the most talented and give them the chance for further study at her school to hone their talents. Cindy chose me, along with a couple of other promising students.

"You need more intense training and the chance to be with strong dancers who can push you," she told me after I'd spent one forty-five-minute class practicing the same basic positions and *pliés.* "You'll get that at my school, and we should start as soon as possible."

I listened politely, but in my heart I didn't feel it. Why in the world would I want to trek across town to study ballet? How would I get there?

I knew I had talent and enjoyed dancing, but I still got a thrill from drill team. I was so excited finally to be following in the footsteps of my big sister, Erica, and Mommy's, too, since she'd once been a Kansas City Chiefs cheerleader. Drill team— *that* was my dream.

Seeing that she was clearly getting nowhere with me, Cindy tried next to enlist my mother, sending home notes expressing how excited she would be to have me as her student. But she chose the wrong messenger. I'd leave the notes that raved about my talent and potential smushed in the back of my Pee Chee folder, or toss them, grease-stained, into the trash, along with my sandwich wrapper and the other remnants of my lunch.

Of course I didn't tell Cindy that her notes were barely surviving my trek home. Instead, I made up excuses—that my mother was busy, or still thinking about it, or not really sure. But Cindy kept pressing, promising me a full scholarship that would pay for my training as well as my attire. I'd have that leotard at last, and she'd even give me a ride from school to her studio each afternoon.

Now I knew I had to tell Mommy. It was like getting an offer for a job you didn't really want but realizing, begrudgingly, that the perks and benefits were probably too good to turn down. I told Cindy that maybe she and my mother should talk and reluctantly gave her our home phone number.

Cindy called that evening. I wasn't sure what Mommy would say. Maybe the twenty-five-minute drive from school each day would turn her off to the idea, I thought. I *hoped*. But right away, Mommy said studying with Cindy could be good for me. Mommy didn't see my nerves or ambivalence, only the opportunity.

"You know, when you were a little girl, you loved ballet," she told me, smiling after she'd gotten off the phone.

"I did?" I asked incredulously, having no memory of even knowing what ballet was before I started taking classes in the Boys and Girls Club gym.

"Yes," my mother said. "I bought you a tutu when you were four or five to wear for Halloween. You didn't want to take it off. You wanted to wear it to school and you'd put it on every afternoon when you got home. You even slept in it. It got so raggedy I finally had to sneak and throw that thing away."

I still didn't know what she was talking about.

"Anyway," Mommy said finally, "Miss Bradley seems to think you've got some potential. Let's give it a try and see how it goes."

And so it began. Sometimes I would hitch a ride across town with Erica, who was now seventeen, and her boyfriend, Jeff, slipping into the backseat of his 1989 white Suzuki

Samurai for the trip to Cindy's ritzy neighborhood. But most days I would ride with Cindy, who would be waiting in front of the school, watching for my tiny frame and big feet to emerge from the crowd.

If I didn't yet feel like a ballerina, I now at least looked like one, thanks to the black leotard, pink tights, and pink slippers my scholarship afforded. Five days a week I'd take my place among students who were much more advanced than those I'd danced beside at the Boys and Girls Club—and I'd try my best to keep up.

Unlike the club gym where we danced on wood, Cindy's studio was the real thing, though, like its founder, it had its quirks.

It was in a shopping center with a glass front that allowed you to gaze right into the small front studio where the youngest students took tap dance. Then there was the back studio, where the ballet company rehearsed. It resembled a box with mirrors—compact and spare. We faced gray walls as we glided across a sprung floor covered in marley. A few tiny dressing rooms and a bathroom were tucked in the corner. And while most ballet classes have an actual pianist providing the musical background, there was no piano at the San Pedro Dance Center, just a portable sound system and a pile of CDs and tapes.

I would get to know every groove of that space over the next three years, spending nearly every day that I wasn't performing, or in a program far away, there, in that studio.

My classmates were mostly white, but there were a few other children of color.

Catalina, who to this day remains one of my best friends,

was Latina, round, loud, and full of light. She would gild her uniform of black and pink with tiny, bright flowers braided into her hair. I was older, but no one would have guessed that because I was so small, barely topping seventy pounds and standing merely a whisper over four feet. Catalina immediately assumed the role of big sister.

"Do you need any help, little girl?" she asked me during my first week at the school, when I was straightening out my leotard in the dressing room.

"No, I'm fine," I answered, giving her a side glance. *Little girl?* "How old are you?" I asked her.

"Ten," she replied.

"Well," I said a bit haughtily, "I'm thirteen." Her almond eyes were disbelieving. But from that day forward, we were rarely ever apart.

Then there was Jason Haley, an African American boy to whom I became very close. Tall, dark, and elegant, Jason was in all my classes at the center and would often be my dance partner. He, too, was a latecomer to ballet, one of Cindy's scholarship students, and a member of the Boys and Girls Club. We had all that in common and much more.

Ballet was a respite in otherwise turbulent lives for the both of us.

Jason had bounced between homes as a child, with his father gone and his mother grappling with poverty. By the time we met, he was living with an aunt. He was gifted and graceful, but raw. You never knew if he would show up for a performance, and he rarely made it to ballet class on time. Eventually, he would drift away from the studio.

But for a while it was we three brown kids, and our

presence reflected Cindy's character and vision. She was different from most people in the ballet world, who felt Giselle and Odette were best performed by dovelike sprites, lissome and ivory-skinned. Cindy believed that ballet was richer when it embraced diverse shapes and colors. There would be times in my career when I would struggle to remember that, but I would eventually come back to that conviction, that the stage on which I performed was brighter for having me, even if some in the audience or dancing beside me didn't always agree.

FOR A WHILE, I was just going through the motions. Then it happened.

I don't recall the precise moment—whether it was during that first week at Cindy's studio, when I found myself immersed in a new world, or weeks later, when my classes at the dance center became as much a daily ritual as my thumping the alarm clock in the dark before dawn.

Maybe it was all that rigor and routine, my dance mates and I lined up perfectly at the barre, like minarets. Maybe it was peering into the mirrored walls reeking of Windex and realizing that the ballerina staring back was graceful, was good, was *me*. What I do remember is that the drill team, the stuff of my elementary-school dreams, faded in importance, and ballet was suddenly thrilling. It was all I wanted—*needed*—to do.

Cindy pushed me from the very start, putting me in an advanced class to see if I could keep up with students who had been training for years. I could, and I did. That was a sign for her to push me even further and faster. Techniques that would normally take a young dancer months, even years, to learn, let alone perfect, I mastered in minutes. Or so Cindy said.

Eight weeks after walking into Cindy's school, I stood *en pointe* for the first time.

Going *en pointe*, wearing reinforced toe shoes that allow a ballerina to dance on the tips of her toes, is a rite of passage for young dancers. I later learned that most budding ballerinas beg their teachers for years even to try pointe shoes on. Once they receive their first pair, they do nothing but simple, repetitive exercises for several more years to adjust to the movements and to make sure their feet are strong enough before they try complex steps: *fouettés, pirouettes, renversés*. Moving too fast is dangerous. Dancers who are not yet ready can seriously damage their feet and impair their performance and technique for years to come, essentially ending their careers before they start.

But Cindy believed that I had the strength and the skill to stand *en pointe* just months after I'd taken my first ballet class. She was so confident, in fact, that she had her camera ready and snapped a picture of that most significant milestone. It's kind of like your mother capturing your baby self at the moment you release her hand and walk for the first time. So many miss it, but not Cindy. I think that from the beginning, in her mind, in her plan, stardom was my destiny, and she was determined to document every turn, step, and breakthrough along the way.

"The perfect ballerina has a small head, sloping shoulders, long legs, big feet, and a narrow rib cage," Cindy said one afternoon, reading George Balanchine's description of the ideal dancer.

She looked up and stared at me, adoringly. "That's you," she said softly. "You're perfect."

I beamed.

"You're going to dance in front of kings and queens," she said. "You will have a life most people cannot even imagine."

I began to believe her.

∞

Chapter 3

BALLET GAVE MY LIFE grace and structure. At the dance center, all the twists and turns were up to me, firmly within my power to master. It was a stark contrast to my life outside, which was spinning out of control.

In the house where we lived with Robert, I shared a beautiful room with Erica and Lindsey; it had a door of stained glass that led to the wide, verdant backyard, where we could dance and play. Life was more rigid than it had been with Harold. There was no laughing with our mouths full, no elbows plopped on the table during dinnertime. We had to be quiet as we ate, though sometimes the struggle to stay silent would make us giggle even more. We'd look at one another, our faces twitching, and finally explode in laughter.

Robert would glare or yell at us to quiet down. He also didn't tolerate Erica's aversion to vegetables. Many a night the rest of us had cleared our plates and were midway through *The Cosby Show* or *Roseanne*, while Erica was still at the dinner table, made to sit there until she'd forced down every carrot and pea.

Still, in some ways his strict rules were comforting for an anxious child like me. And I later appreciated the order we'd briefly had in our home, in contrast to the instability that would define our lives when we moved away from Robert.

Like our years with Harold, we never wanted for anything. There was plenty of food in the refrigerator, closets bursting with matching outfits, and toys and books all around.

And since Mommy never was much of a cook, Robert was the family chef. He made sure all of us kids felt at home in the kitchen, teaching us how to boil rice from scratch instead of heating the instant stuff that came in a box.

I began to spend more time with him than my brothers and sisters did. Since I was a people pleaser, I'd volunteer to accompany him when he ran errands, picking up tools or wax to buff his beloved Jeep. After a while, Robert would come looking for me.

"Grab your piggy bank and come for a ride," he'd whisper.

We'd drive to the grocery store, and while he browsed, picking up fruit and cold cuts, I'd spend my dimes and quarters on Snickers bars, cookies, and sunflower seeds.

"Hey, little Hawaiian girl," he'd sing when he came home from work and saw me playing with my Barbie. Robert also had big dreams for me. He thought I would make a great jockey because I was so tiny.

"We should get you horse-riding lessons," he told me. "You're small and don't weigh a lot, like the best folks out there riding. It's a very prestigious sport. Have you ever heard of the Kentucky Derby?"

He often remarked on how much I looked like him and his relatives. It's true that I probably looked more Polynesian or Asian than my brothers and sisters, with my almond-shaped eyes and long brown hair. I began to realize that my appearance made all the difference in the world to Robert and some others in his family.

It was clear I was Robert's favorite, and that led to a new riff in the good-natured but relentless teasing that was as much a part of our family sound track as Mariah Carey's latest hit or the theme to *Monday Night Football*.

"Stop it," I'd yell at Doug Jr. when he playfully snatched a book out of my hands.

"What are you going to do?" he'd ask, holding the book behind his back. "Tell Robert?"

"Yes!" I'd yell back.

But I seldom did. I loved my big brother. And Robert had a bad temper.

I WAS CLOSE TO Robert's mother, Grandma Marie. In the summer, when school was out, Mommy would drop me off at her small stucco home, and I'd help Grandma Marie tend to the smaller children who came to the day-care center she ran in her house. She was the one who taught me how to sew, and I felt like quite the artist, tugging on my shiny needle to create outfits for my dolls.

After a while, I began to notice that while I often went to Robert's parents' house, my brothers and sisters were rarely invited. And Robert's father, Grandpa Martin, was a shadow to us, sullen-faced and holed up in his room on the rare occasions our entire family stopped by. I don't think he ever spoke to, or even acknowledged, any of us kids.

Back at our house, my being Robert's favorite didn't spare me from his discipline. Like my siblings I'd have to go silently stand in the corner if I didn't make up my bed or if I made too much noise. But we girls didn't have to go to the corner as often or for as long as Doug and Chris. They'd be made to stare at the crease in the wall for an hour or more, usually while balancing a heavy book on their heads. It was painful for them—and painful for me to watch.

When Robert was growing up, it wasn't uncommon for his father to hit him. Robert was thrust into the role of fathering five kids, and I think he was trying to raise the boys the way he'd been brought up. He was hard on my brothers, especially Chris, who was rambunctious and loud.

Once when Chris was boiling the rice for dinner, he burned the grains into a thick crust in the bottom of the pot. Robert literally dragged him back to the kitchen by his ear. "Clean it up!" he screamed, and Chris quickly obeyed. Another time, for an infraction I can no longer remember, Robert hit Chris with a frying pan.

Sometimes Robert encouraged violence rather than inflicting it.

Chris and Doug were arguing with each other one Saturday like they often did, this time about whose football team would have a better season.

"The Forty-Niners!" Chris shouted.

"You must be crazy," Doug yelled. "Do you know what Randall Cunningham has done for the Eagles this year?"

Suddenly, Robert intervened. "Since you guys can't agree, you'll have to fight it out."

Robert made the boys walk behind him out to the backyard. Then he got some of the rags he used to buff his Jeep from inside the garage. He wrapped my brothers' fists.

"Now," Robert screamed. "Fight!"

It was an awful ritual that we'd see again and again, a battle royal that seemed designed to showcase his power over us all. Mommy would stand to the side, watching and crying. But she never stopped it. The fight would usually end when one of my brothers would say he gave up and both were in tears.

We grew to be terrified of Robert. When we heard his Jeep barreling around the corner, rumbling into the long driveway, we'd scramble, picking up toys, straightening up magazines, afraid that if the house wasn't clean and organized the way Robert liked it, there would be hell to pay. Erica began to spend the night at a friend's house as often as she could. And Doug and Chris spent a lot of time in their room.

I'd often join my brothers there, crawling into Doug's top bunk, where we'd listen to tapes of New Edition, or the latest rhymes from MC Hammer and LL Cool J.

"Mr. Telephone Man, there's something wrong with my line." Doug and I would bop our heads to the beat. We felt safe there together, just us and our music.

But we could avoid Robert for only so long, and we didn't have to do much to make him angry. And though he was tough on the boys for acting out, Lindsey didn't have to do anything at all to earn his wrath.

Lindsey, our baby sister, was the spitting image of her father, Harold, with skin the color of caramelized butter and a tight tuft of dark brown curls. She looked more African American than any of our mixed-race clan, and it seemed that whenever there was a glass broken, a toy in the middle of the floor, or too much yelling on a Sunday morning, Lindsey was always, *always* to blame.

Often, when he was angry, he would call Lindsey a nigger.

It stunned me. That was a word I'd heard only in black-and-white documentaries about the bad old South. I knew it was a terrible thing to call my baby sister.

We'd hear that slur and many more often over the next few years. The Arab guy at the store was a "sand nigger." Robert talked about smelly Indians. He'd use the N word when a black man cut him off on the freeway and talk about spics when he saw Latino teenagers hanging out on the playground.

Things just got worse between Robert and Mommy. She began to confide in us kids, telling us stories about Robert's family that we really had no business hearing. Like how they didn't believe our baby brother Cameron was Robert's child, though by the time Cameron's newborn smoothness disappeared and his features came into focus, it was clear he was the mirror image of his father.

Looking back, it's clear that Robert's family didn't trust my mother. And as hateful as some of them were, in some ways I don't blame them. Robert had a comfortable life on his own, and then all of a sudden this woman moved in with her five children. She was older than him, still married to another man, and they lived together a year and a half and had a baby before they finally headed to City Hall and became husband and wife. It was all very shady, and now, with the perspective that comes with distance and time, I can understand why they were wary.

But it was shocking to realize that for certain of them the *main* reason for hating my mother, for not wanting my brothers and sisters even to visit, seemed to be because we were black. It was the first time I'd felt any negativity because of the way my family looked or because of what we were.

Deep down, I believe Robert had to have had a good heart to marry a woman who had five children and—at least initially—to treat each of them like his own. He was also the father of my beloved baby brother Cameron, and I think he wanted to make his marriage work—for us to be a family. But there was such negativity and bigotry in his family, I think he succumbed to the pressure, and the ugliness that he'd grown up with began to ooze out of him as well.

I'd see bigotry again and again in my ballet career, and it would hurt every time. But after living with Robert it would no longer come as a surprise.

Like when I moved to New York when I was sixteen, and the other ballerinas would look at me, not sure that I was black but certain I wasn't white, and proceed to ignore me.

Or when I tried out for six ballet companies' summer programs, received invitations from all but one, and Cindy told me that the one rejection was because of the color of my skin.

"Save it," Cindy told me, referring to the curt turndown that had come in the mail. "One day, they'll be sorry."

I don't know if they ever were. But I still have that letter.

MOMMY STARTED COMPLAINING MORE and more about Robert.

"He's got his nerve talking about folks," she'd say. "Lots of people don't like Asians, either."

Or "He'd better watch his mouth. One day he's going to call somebody a name, they'll hear him, and he's going to wind up beat down to the ground."

But that was all muttered behind Robert's back. When he was home, screaming at us, making the boys fight, repeating a racist joke and howling with laughter, she'd say nothing. She'd nervously look down at her lap, like there was some safe harbor there. But she wouldn't rebuke him. She wouldn't protect us. We kids were on our own.

Sometimes when Robert wanted Mommy to hurry up and clean the bathroom or get Cameron dressed, he would grab her by the arm and yank her. I began to see bruises peeking out from beneath the camisole she wore under her blouse.

About four years after we'd moved in with Robert, my mother told us kids that she was beginning to fear for her life. And so in the fifth month of my first year at Dana Middle School, it was again time to pick up and go.

A few weeks before we left, Mommy huddled us all together.

"We've got to get out of here," Mommy said, practically whispering, though Robert had gone out. "Robert can't have a hint that we're leaving. When it's time, I'll let you know. Be ready."

Mommy could be very dramatic. If the situation wasn't so tense, it might even have been comical or fun. I could almost pretend we were actors in a spy flick, or co-conspirators planning our escape from a penal colony.

Erica, Doug, and Chris had never really liked Robert. They

were devoted to Harold, whom we considered our real father (and whom we'd still see on many weekends). Years of being subjected to Robert's yelling, name-calling, and sometimes violence had curdled my siblings' dislike of him into hatred. Now that our getaway was being planned, they'd smirk when he screamed, knowing that they wouldn't have to put up with it much longer. Mommy, too, would give us a knowing glance, almost a wink, during Robert's tirades. Then she'd return her gaze to her lap and proceed to do whatever Robert told her to do.

One morning Robert got in his Jeep and headed to his office as usual. Mommy would usually leave about half an hour after he did and head to her job at an office products company.

But not today.

Lindsey, Erica, and I were buttoning our shirts and combing our hair when Mommy burst into our room and told us that we weren't going to school.

"Today's the day," she said breathlessly.

We broke into a sprint, grabbing suitcases and stuffing them with whatever we could carry. With baby Cameron, there were seven of us now, but in most other ways we were leaving Robert's home the way we had come, urgently, and with little more than the clothes on our backs.

About an hour later, a car pulled up in front of the house. There was a knock on the door.

"It's time to go," Mommy said, opening it.

Standing there was a tall, skinny white guy with wire-rimmed glasses and tousled brown hair. I'd never seen him before. He began carrying our suitcases to a Toyota I later learned he'd borrowed from a friend. It was parked behind Mommy's gray Chevy Corsica.

"That's Ray," Mommy said hastily, filling her trunk with bags. Though the mysterious Ray was clearly playing a role in our escape, no one wanted to ride with him. Instead, we kids crowded into our mother's car.

Mommy got behind the wheel, and my brothers, sisters, and I rounded those mountainous bends that seemed to leap toward the Pacific Ocean one last time.

I LOVE MY MOTHER, but I've never really understood her.

She was beautiful. Like Mariah, our mother had a flood of chestnut curls cascading down her back. Mommy's locks were flecked with ruby and gold, and they formed a halo of ringlets around her deep brown eyes and sandstone skin.

She and Mariah Carey could have been sisters. That much was clear. Maybe that's why our family loved the golden-locked singer so much. Erica would one day name her only daughter after her. And we played Mariah Carey's debut album almost as much as we watched sports. "Vision of Love" was even my baby brother's lullaby. Cameron would cry until he heard Mariah's five-octave voice; when we popped in Mariah's CD, he would curl up in his crib and fall fast asleep.

Wherever Mommy went, she was bound to be the prettiest woman in the room, and I would beam, waiting for everyone to realize that the beauty in their midst was *my* mother. She was impeccable, too, refusing even to walk to the mailbox without a swipe of coral lipstick or sweep of mascara.

Mommy always worked, usually in sales, though she'd been trained as a nurse back in Kansas City. After getting off work in the early evening, she'd drive to the Boys and Girls Club to pick up us kids. I think everyone there looked forward to hearing the staccato of her high heels clicking across the hardwood floors. They waited to greet her, from the teenage boy spiking a ball who would pause to give her a goofy grin to the male counselors who'd put their phone calls on hold, smooth their hair, and inevitably poke their heads out their office doors so they could say hello.

My brothers hated all the attention, especially Doug Jr. "Stay in the car and we'll come out," he'd grumble angrily just about every day. But she didn't listen. I think the sweet asides felt too good. They were balms on tough days, a respite from what had too often been a tough, tragic life.

She wasn't long out of high school when she married her first husband, Mike, who had a sky-high afro, Hershey-kissed skin, and a love for all things basketball. But a bullet took away his hoop dreams and all the other plans he and Mommy may have had for the future. He and Mommy had gone to Oakland, California, to help his younger brother, who they were afraid was involved in drugs, and Mike was shot and killed.

My mother cried and mourned with his best friend, Doug, and a year later they got married. That man, Doug Copeland, was my father.

I know that to survive such a childhood took resilience, and I always figured that my mother's near-constant sorrow and loss helped fuel her devotion to my brothers, sisters, and me. With us, she had a family that wouldn't fade away, that she could always carry with her. But as our lives began to repeat the rootlessness that had haunted her own itinerant childhood, I wondered why. Knowing what she had gone through, why didn't she try harder to give us the stability she herself must have craved? I wanted to claim her perseverance as my emotional inheritance, not her dependence on men, or her frantic getaways into the night.

When we first left Robert, we went to stay in downtown L.A. with friends of our mother's. Auntie Monique and Uncle Charles, as we called them, were wonderful, opening up their small home to Mommy, my siblings, and me. But despite their hospitality, my usual, everyday anxieties took a backseat to a fear of real, palpable danger, just as they had on Robert's worst days.

I'd never lived in a place like this before. Auntie Monique and Uncle Charles's neighborhood was Crips turf, the battleground of one of L.A.'s most infamous gangs. The men wore blue do-rags to pledge their allegiance to one violent faction or the other and scrawled their graffiti on fences and stop signs.

The Kansas City Chiefs decal Mommy sported in her car window seemed to agitate some of the gang members. The L.A. Raiders were a big deal in the city, unsurprisingly, but besides the tension football could cause among gang members, the Chief's color was a bright Bloods red. All I really know is that they would give us hard looks as we rode by, and we worried about a bullet piercing the windshield every time Mommy drove us home from school.

We were right to. One evening we were in the living room watching television. There was the *pop, pop* of gunfire, then footsteps, and a heavy thud on Uncle Charles and Auntie Monique's front porch.

We ran outside. A man, probably in his early twenties, was writhing in pain, blood spreading like an inkblot on his blue jeans.

"I'm hit," he sputtered weakly.

Auntie Monique ran inside to call 911 while Uncle Charles shouted orders.

"Get some water," he yelled. I ran inside, shoved a pot under the kitchen faucet, then ran back to the porch, water spilling onto the carpet along with my tears.

"What's that?" Uncle Charles asked incredulously, cradling the wounded stranger's head and looking at me as if I was crazy not to understand what the victim of a drive-by shooting needed as he waited for an ambulance. "The man is thirsty! He needs some water to drink." I ran back in the house and grabbed a glass, feeling shaken and helpless.

I can't remember what happened to that man, if he lived or died. We stayed with Auntie Monique and Uncle Charles for several weeks more, and when Mommy told us we were leaving, I was glad for once to be moving on. But my relief was short-lived.

It turned out that we were moving in with Ray, Mommy's new boyfriend, whom none of us kids could stand. He was a nerd who tried entirely too hard to be cool, blasting Ice Cube and EPMD from morning till night.

"Yo, Doug! Erica! Pete Rock and CL Smooth just dropped a new jam," he'd say. "Come hear it."

Erica would roll her eyes and go back to reading a magazine. Doug would get a look on his face like he was ready to explode and go outside to practice his dribbling.

Mommy also started to change in a way that unnerved us all. Instead of being our stern, if exuberant, mother, she seemed to revert to some version of her teenage self. She and Ray got matching tattoos of each other's name swirled in black ink on their shoulders. And Mommy would kiss Ray passionately in front of us, something she had never done with Harold or Robert. It made us sick.

My older siblings had begun to grow bitter toward Mommy when we lived with Robert, and now I started to get the same sour taste in my mouth. We wanted a mother who was responsible, who either stayed married or stayed single, and who put her children before some random man. In our sports-obsessed family we couldn't understand how many marriages she had to fumble, how many relationships she had to lose, before she got out of the game. We couldn't understand why she needed a man at all—why we children were never enough.

Ray worked at the office products company with Mommy, but didn't seem to earn much. Mommy worked in sales, but her commissions ebbed and flowed. Robert had been the real breadwinner. So now money was tight. We subsisted on Top Ramen noodles, potato chips, and soda pop, with an occasional can of vegetables thrown in. Mommy had never been much of a cook, rarely touching the stove. And again, she seemed content to shirk her responsibilities, giving Doug or Erica a few dollars culled from her paycheck or Ray's to go grocery shopping. Then Chris—who had been Robert's best student in the kitchen but was barely fifteen—would prepare the family meals, whipping up tacos or spaghetti from a couple of pounds of ground beef that he stretched as far as he could.

We stayed with Ray for about a year before moving even farther away from our onetime home in San Pedro to a town called Montebello, where we lived in another cramped apartment with Mommy's next boyfriend, Alex. He was Latino and seemed a little more at ease in his own skin than Ray, but he wasn't much more stable. We were never sure if Alex had a real job. And just like at Ray's, Mommy and Alex slept in the one bedroom while we kids spread blankets and pillows wherever we could find a clear spot on the living room floor.

The neighborhoods where Ray and Alex lived weren't dicey like the streets where Auntie Monique and Uncle Charles lived, but their apartments were meant as basic, temporary housing for young men who partied all night and woke up at noon, not for a family with six children. And in those cramped spaces, the scraping back of a kitchen chair or the ringing of the telephone seemed louder, as if the smallness and clutter amplified the sound.

We were coming undone. Mommy had always been a neat freak, but there were too many people and too little room to bother tidying up much. And she no longer wore her high heels and stylish suits. She had no reason to. Sometime between living with Ray and then Alex, Mommy had lost her last job and was struggling to find a new one. Our gray Chevy Corsica was gone now, too.

We kids were still a unified tribe, more so now than ever. I was never alone in riding the bus or walking home. But the distance between us and Mommy continued to grow.

Then, a few months after we began living with Alex, he lost his apartment. Again, we moved, this time into a motel. He came with us.

It was called the Sunset Inn, two stories of stucco just off a busy highway. We were now in Gardena, a town right next to San Pedro. We were closer to our old neighborhood, but this place, this part of town, didn't feel like home.

Our room was toward the back of the top story. We children

slept on the couch and the floor in the large front room, but I would often disappear into Mommy's bedroom after school, trying to drift away in a dream or a dance. Our front porch looking out over the Pacific was long gone, replaced by an outdoor hallway that we and the other motel tenants shared.

I tried to make the best of it. I would pretend the hallway was a veranda and I'd sit there, soaking up the sun. And I turned the rail into my very own barre, which I would grab hold of to balance as I stretched toward the sky. Or I would place Cameron's tiny hands on the cool metal and shift him into various ballet positions, the way Cindy had first done with me.

Cameron was in and out of our lives at that point. His father, Robert, didn't want him living in a motel, so he took Mommy to court and was given primary custody. Cameron would be with us only on weekends. It devastated me. Cameron's absence in my life opened a wound in my heart. Now I didn't hold back the emotions that hurt me. The tears that poured out of all of us when we had to say good-bye are still fresh in my gut and memory to this day. It was like nothing I'd ever experienced—I wasn't ever this expressive of my pain when we left Doug Senior or Harold or Robert, but Cameron was my baby. I think all of us kids felt we had contributed to raising him. I continued to see Cameron at Robert's home if he wasn't at the motel on weekends, but it simply wasn't the same, especially when my other siblings' presence in my life was likewise beginning to fracture. Lindsey had always spent weeks at a time with Harold, her father. And Erica, who had started staying with friends as much as she could back when we lived with Robert, now hardly ever slept at home. Our family, fraying even at the best of times, was now unraveling.

Often we had no money at all. We would run our hands around the couch cushions and through the carpet to find change. Then we'd go to the corner store to see if we could afford something to eat. Eventually, Mommy applied for food stamps.

I still tried to appear perfect at school, arriving long before the first bell, carrying out my duties as hall monitor and as leader of the drill team. I withdrew even more inside myself as I tried to keep it all a secret, not telling my friends that we'd moved again, that I didn't have my own room . . . let alone a bed. I'd always spent more time at my friends' homes than they'd spent at mine, so it wasn't that hard to pretend my life was as it should be.

It was harder to make myself forget. I was grateful to hide from the chaos for a little while at the dance studio, inside ballet, where there were rules and life was dignified. Beautiful. I had continued to go to the studio every day despite the turmoil at home, taking the half hour drive with Cindy from school, and then riding an hour on the bus to get home to the motel.

The weeks rushed by. My mastery of ballet deepened, and soon I had my first show. It was at the Palos Verdes Art Center and billed as an "afternoon of art, music, and cultural enrichment," performed for a mostly elderly and white audience of about two hundred.

On the program was an older teenage girl who sang some forgettable pop standard, a group of high schoolers who performed a modern-dance routine, and me, the only ballerina in the bunch. Cindy had created a simple routine that blended the positions, spins, and leaps that I had managed to learn up to that point. I wore my black leotard with a pink chiffon skirt, with a blush-colored rose tucked in my hair.

Mommy wasn't there. Neither were my brothers or sisters. Only Cindy.

But I had performed ballet solo in front of a crowd for the first time, and by then I was in love. It was fun, exciting—and each day I couldn't wait for the bell to ring after sixth period so I could rush out the door, jump into Cindy's car, and head to the studio.

Mommy, however, was starting to change her mind about my ballet dreams.

When Jeff couldn't give her a lift, Erica would catch the bus, riding an hour each way to pick me up from class so I wouldn't have to take public transportation by myself. The two of us would get home after dark, often exhausted.

One night after Erica and I returned home from our long trek from the studio, Mommy sat down beside me. She said ballet class, so far away, wasn't working out.

"It's too much," she said, shaking her head, sadness faintly clouding her eyes. "You need to be able to get home earlier to spend time with your brothers and sisters. And both you and Erica are missing out on time with your friends. I know you're liking this class, but you'll only be a kid once."

I knew that Mommy meant well, that she was speaking from a place of concern, but I don't think she really understood that for me, ballet had become more than a hobby—it was what helped me stand alone, even shine bright. I desperately needed it.

The day after Mommy told me I would have to quit ballet, Cindy was waiting for me in front of the school, rifling through her organizer, looking up from time to time to see if I'd appeared.

I opened the car door and got in beside her.

"I'm going to have to stop dancing," I blurted out before breaking down in tears. "My mother says that the studio's too far. That it's too much, that I'm missing out on time with my friends and family."

Perhaps she would have been better able to understand if, like many concerned parents of ballerinas, my mother had been worried about my struggling schoolwork or fatigue. But this excuse seemed flimsy, even to me.

Cindy looked as though she'd forgotten how to breathe. Her eyes were wide and glistening. We sat there for a few minutes, silent.

"Well then," she finally said, "at least I can drive you home."

I was too tired to protest, too grief-stricken to guard my secret. I gave her my address.

We were quiet in the car. I tried to imagine what would fill the space that ballet had occupied, and I kept coming up empty. Finally, Cindy pulled to a stop. Staring at the run-down motel where my family was living, she looked as stunned as she had when I told her that I couldn't dance with her anymore.

"Thanks for the ride," I whispered as I hurried out of the car. Upstairs, I fumbled for the room key and entered the living room, blankets rolled up near the spots where they would later be unfurled as makeshift beds.

I'm sure Mommy didn't believe she was being neglectful. After all, we hadn't always lived that way, with pallets on the floor. We hadn't always called a motel—with a lobby window to slide our rent check through—home. We didn't always sleep around the corner from a highway lined with liquor stores and sketchy taco joints.

But that's how we lived now. That's what Cindy saw.

There was a knock on the door. Mommy, who'd been in the bedroom with Alex, came out and opened it.

Cindy stood there tentatively. I could feel the tension building in the small space, a nearly tangible thing. I just wanted to disappear. She met my eyes where I sat withdrawn on the floor. I believe that she knew this was it: she either brought me with her that night and into the world she believed I was born to be a part of, or I would never dance again.

The two women huddled a while, talking softly, crying, too. Mommy made it very clear that she had five other children. I was not, nor could I be, the center of her universe. I knew that—but I needed to be that to someone. "I can't leave her," Cindy said, tears steaming down her face. "I want Misty to come live with me." Then Mommy sighed and looked around the crowded motel room.

And she let me go.

Chapter 4

66

∞

IT WAS LATE WHEN we pulled up to Cindy's house.

When Mommy said I could leave, I was in a daze but managed somehow to stuff my world into a backpack. Blue jeans, pajamas, a few tops. By then I didn't have very much. Then she hugged me tight, and I walked slowly out of one kind of life and into another.

Cindy lived across town near the Angel's Gate Lighthouse in a condominium perched on a hill. Her husband, Patrick, was a full-time art teacher. But in his spare time, he loved to surf. When he wasn't catching waves or teaching dance at the San Pedro Dance Studio, he was baking desserts. Their front door was barely two blocks from Cabrillo Beach, and the condo smelled like cinnamon and the sea. It was filled with paintings, sculptures, and other tiny beautiful things. I remember thinking that nothing so fragile could ever have survived in my home.

As we walked through the door, Cindy said, "Misty is here

with me. She's going to be living with us. Can you set a third place setting at the table?"

"Sure thing," Patrick said, not even missing a beat.

I know now that Cindy never asked him for permission or even let him know I was coming. They welcomed me with the most generous and open arms. We ate Chinese food that night at the dinner table, like I had always been there.

After dinner, Cindy led me to the large bedroom that I would share with her three-year-old son Wolf, whom I'd often seen at the studio, taking tap dance. He was asleep in the bottom bunk. I changed my clothes, climbed into the top bed, and she came to tuck me in.

"Good night, honey," she whispered as she kissed me on the cheek. "I'm so glad you're here."

As sudden as it all was—Mommy's consent, my moving out of the motel room we'd shared—I knew that my going to live with my dance instructor was not an unusual arrangement. Talented young dancers and athletes often leave home to live with their coaches and teachers so they can concentrate on training. Even Cindy had moved out of her childhood home as a teenager to pursue a dance career.

Still, I lay in the dark, terrified. Now I would have to try to fit in not only at school but also in this new home. It was yet another test to pass, another social maze to figure my way through.

But I also knew how devastated I'd been when I'd found out I wasn't going to be able to do ballet anymore, how the hurt had stung my soul.

"So I guess this is it," I told myself. "This is how I'm going to be able to continue to dance." I had to accept it. Finally, I fell asleep.

When I woke up the next morning, Wolfie was peering over the edge of my bed as he stood on his, gazing at me wide-eyed. He would often look at me that way in the two years that I lived in his room. He seemed ever in awe of this older brown girl who had suddenly appeared in his life. I remember waking up sometimes and finding him softly touching my face in the middle of the night. Wolfie just adored me—and I adored him. He was my new baby brother.

That's how natural it all was. Transitions in my life had always been traumatic. Leaving Harold to move in with Robert, fleeing Robert for Ray, ending up in a motel with my family and Alex. But not this time, not this move. Cindy and Patrick were so welcoming, so warm, and having Wolfie there reminded me of my younger siblings Cameron and Lindsey, whom I loved so much. I didn't have to struggle to fit in after all. The Bradleys embraced me just as I was.

❧

I NO LONGER RODE a public bus to get to Dana Middle School or to get home in the evenings. Cindy would drop me at school in the morning and then pick me up after the last bell rang so that I could head to her studio. I was still captain of the drill team, and I headed to practice every afternoon during my sixth-period PE class, but my interest had waned. The routines now seemed uninspired and simplistic, nothing like ballet, where the movements rippled like water, where a spin that blended strength and grace could transform a dull room into a music box, and the dancer became the beautiful miniature turning round and round inside.

Elizabeth Cantine understood. She was the drill team's coach, but she had seen that I had the lines and fluidity to be a ballerina from the first days of practice. She was the one who'd encouraged me to take Cindy's class at the Boys and Girls Club, and for years to come she would play a vital role in both my budding career and in my life more generally.

I didn't know it at first, but when Cindy offered me the scholarship to attend her school, she had already had a discussion with her friend Elizabeth, and Elizabeth and her husband, Richard, had agreed to help pay for my supplies. That was no small undertaking. Pointe shoes cost eighty dollars a pair, and I ran through them the way a basketball player exhausts his sneakers. I was also still growing, so there was the constant need for new tights and leotards. Elizabeth and Richard would help me financially for many more years. That's how much they believed in and cared for me.

Elizabeth became one of my many mentors, and by the time I was in high school, she and her husband had declared themselves my honorary godparents. She observed my classes at Cindy's school and never missed any of my performances. I would often spend the night at her home, and she remained in my life long after Cindy and I were forced to part. To this day, I still see Elizabeth and Richard, my godparents, often.

I ALWAYS SAY THERE are no shortcuts in ballet, no way to skip steps. That was certainly my truth. You had to know how to do a *plié*—bending your knees over your toes gracefully— and a *passé*—passing your foot above and behind your knee, then back again—before you could whip your leg around in a *fouetté*.

So I started from the bottom at the San Pedro Dance Center, with the babies (as I dubbed the youngest students), though I was so small that most onlookers wouldn't have been able to tell that I was nearly fourteen and years older than my classmates.

In that most basic of classes, we would hold on to the barre with both hands as we practiced *pliés* and went over the most elemental ballet positions. First, second, third, fourth, fifth.

Then it was on to pointe class, where we'd do the same steps we'd practiced at the barre, but elevated to the tips of our toes. I was taking three classes a day, each more advanced than the one before. There were maybe twenty students in each group—most of them girls, most of them white. The classes moved so quickly that half the time I didn't know what the steps with their complex French names and odd spellings were called.

But Cindy threw me into those more advanced classes from the start because she believed I could immediately pick up what was going on around me. I just needed to watch the ballet instructor, or the videos he or she would play, or the other students.

I remember when I began learning how to do those *fouetté* turns. I was always so eager for that class, so excited to try that complicated move again and again, figuring out how to make it better, how to make it work. Cindy taught me how to do it by holding on to the barre, breaking it down into little steps.

"Now you *plié*," she'd explain. "Now swing your leg to the side. Then bring it into *passé*."

I'd repeat those steps every day for an hour, holding on to the barre until I was finally able to let go and make those turns in the center of the room. The day that I was finally able to do it—*plié! relevé! passé!*—was exhilarating.

Then, the next day, it was back to basics, where I would polish what I had learned in the more advanced classes, making sure that every step, every *port de bras* was as pristine as it could be. Learning to dance with a partner, a *pas de deux*, was a class unto itself.

Sometimes Patrick taught the class, but my usual instructor, and my first partner, was Charles Maple. He had been a soloist with ABT.

I was so small and fearless that I became the student he would dance with to teach all the others.

"Hold your body and don't move," he'd say, as he lifted me over his head with one arm. I could be as still as a statue or as flexible as a rag doll—whatever he needed me to be—as he tossed, lifted, and twirled me around. I would end the class giddy and out of breath.

I wasn't really aware of how quickly I was learning. But I began to hear a word over and over again—from Cindy, from Charles, from Elizabeth—that would follow me, define me.

Prodigy.

Initially, I didn't understand that word's magnitude, how it meant that the instinctive space from which I started would be the standard many expected me to maintain. All I knew then, at the beginning, was that dancing was fun, natural. And my constant quest to please pushed me to keep getting better.

All these years later, my technique is very secure, clean, and strong. Yet I still go to ballet classes daily. Dancers understand.

It's because, while we know we'll never achieve perfection, we have to keep trying. Dancers have to keep studying, practicing, and striving until the day they retire.

It's what makes ballet so beautiful, that razor's edge of timing and technique that is the difference between leaping and landing perfectly, or collapsing to the floor.

Human frailty prevents perfection. Your body is forever giving in to fatigue or injury. Something is always a little off. And as your body ages, as the sprains and stresses of life become indelible pieces of your being, your dance technique must change as well. As Misty the woman has grown, so has Misty the ballerina, adjusting to new realities and sudden limitations.

But if you've never walked in a pair of pointe shoes, it's hard to understand.

"You're still taking ballet class?" a childhood friend once asked me incredulously.

The question used to make me weary. But no more.

"Yes," I answered. "I'll be taking ballet classes forever."

∽

BALLET SUFFUSED MY NEW home life as well. I discovered American Ballet Theatre as I was sitting in front of the television in Cindy and Patrick's family room.

Other than music videos, I had never seen professional dancing of any kind—let alone ballet. But at Cindy's it was pretty much all we watched. Gone were the Sunday afternoon football games that had dominated my family life. At the Bradleys, I would sit in front of the TV for hours watching videotaped performances by ABT. I was mesmerized, the same way I had been when I discovered gymnastics. Only it wasn't Nadia Comaneci on the screen. It was Gelsey Kirkland, Natalia Makarova, Rudolf Nureyev, and Paloma Herrera.

ABT was founded in 1940. Based in New York, it quickly became known as one of the finest classical ballet companies in the world. Cindy and Patrick knew that. And they saw it as my destiny.

Mikhail Baryshnikov became ABT's artistic director in 1980. But just a few years earlier, he was a performer, at Wolf Trap. It was a tour de force. He and Gelsey Kirkland, the famed ballerina of the 1960s and 1970s and one of George Balanchine's muses, danced the *pas de deux* from *Don Quixote*, and I watched the videotape of their performance perhaps a hundred times. It was then that I decided that I wanted to be Kitri.

In *Don Quixote*, Kitri was the innkeeper's daughter, sensual and full of fire, refusing to marry the wealthy nobleman and wanting instead to be with Basilio, the barber. She communicates her sass and spunk with every move, gently turning her torso while tipping one shoulder—an *épaulement*—all the while seductively opening, closing, and waving her beautiful fan.

With a simple flick of the wrist, or the childish stomping of her feet when she is being forced to marry someone she doesn't want, she oozes attitude. The ballet is full of quick, explosive footwork, as well as fierce, large jumps. But the choreography is only part of it. The dancer must take on Kitri's personality, must *become* her, to convey the tale successfully.

I don't know why I saw myself in Kitri. I just felt a connection.

Gelsey Kirkland made me fall in love with Kitri, and it was through Kitri that I discovered Paloma.

Paloma Herrera was one of the youngest stars in the history of ABT. Born in Buenos Aires, she was fifteen when she joined its corps de ballet, seventeen when she was promoted to soloist, and nineteen when she became a principal dancer. She became my idol, and I followed her the way other teenagers obsessed over Winona Ryder's next movie or Madonna's newest love affair. The first time I ever saw *Don Quixote* performed live at the Dorothy Chandler Pavilion in downtown Los Angeles, Paloma was the star.

She had just been promoted to principal and was playing Kitri to Angel Corella's Basilio. At that time, the two of them were the hottest thing in ballet. They were both young, beautiful, and Latin—and ideal for those roles. Cindy and I went to see them together, and I remember sitting in my seat stunned, starstruck.

I followed Paloma's career for years, collecting articles about her in *Dance* and *Pointe* magazines, as well as the *New York Times*. The luxury watch company Movado was also a sponsor of ABT, and Paloma's visage graced their ads.

I was desperate to follow Paloma's path. I, too, had to join a major dance company as soon as I could, and I resolved that by the time other girls were picking out their dresses for senior prom, I would be a principal dancer taking the lead in *Romeo and Juliet* or *La Bayadère*.

Of course, that made no sense. I had come to ballet too late to be a soloist or principal before I exited my teens. What Paloma had done was rare even for ballerinas like her, those who had danced their entire lives.

Four years later, when I was seventeen and had joined ABT, I would meet Paloma. We would share a stage and become good friends. But long before we were peers, she was everything to me.

WHILE BALLET WAS THE center of my life with Cindy, it was only one part. The rigors of ballet, classes, rehearsals, and a growing number of performances were cushioned by the warm rituals of family life.

This was new for me. I'd experienced structure when I lived with Robert, but that had been accompanied by violence and fear. The routines at the Bradleys left me feeling protected and loved.

I don't know if Cindy and Patrick were exactly wealthy. But based on what I had been exposed to, they definitely seemed well-off financially, and stable. When I did my homework, it was against a backdrop of stillness and quiet. I even had a family pet for the first time, a little black poodle named Misha that Cindy had named after Mikhail Baryshnikov.

Not long after I moved in with them, Cindy, Patrick, Wolfie, and I went to a photo studio and had family portraits taken. The pictures of us—me in a black leotard, and Wolfie in a pint-size Danskin—were perched all over the house. We had become a family.

When I met Cindy's parents, Catherine and Irving, they told me to call them "Bubby" and "Papa," just like Wolfie did. We spent so much time in each other's home that, when Bubby and Papa eventually bought a house around the corner, Wolfie and I each had our own room there.

I also began to learn the rites and traditions of Judaism, Cindy's faith.

Growing up, there had been many Sundays when Harold would drive to Robert's, scoop up my brothers, sisters, and me, and take us to church. But I was Christian primarily in an "it's Easter, it's Christmas, let's go to service" kind of way.

Now, I occasionally went to temple with Bubby and Papa. And every Friday we would dine together to celebrate Shabbat, lighting candles before sundown and reciting the special prayers:

Baruch atah, Adonai, Eloheinu, melech haolam
(Blessed are you, Lord, our God,
sovereign of the universe)
asher kid'shanu b'mitzvotav v'tzivanu
(who has sanctified us with His
commandment and commanded us)
l'hadlik ner shel Shabbat.
(to light the lights of Shabbat.)
Amein
(Amen)

I came to know those words by heart.

I was also back in the kitchen, like I'd been with Robert, but now Bubby was the master chef, and I was learning how to make matzo ball soup. We'd stir the matzo meal, eggs, water, and chicken fat in a large bowl, then spoon the mixture to make big dumplings. I'd drop them into a pot of bubbling hot broth and watch them float to the top.

Finally, I thought to myself. *This is what a family is supposed to be like.*

There were no other blacks at the synagogue we attended. But I know that only from the snapshot of my memory. It wasn't something I really noticed at the time, though perhaps Bubby did.

One Saturday, when I was visiting her and we had finished puttering around the kitchen, Bubby put a cassette in the VCR. It was *To Sir, with Love*, the 1967 film starring the legendary black actor Sidney Poitier as a teacher trying to educate a group of mostly white children in the slums of London.

We watched it together, and when it ended, Bubby sang along with the theme song, softly.

"He was the first black man to win an Oscar," she said of Poitier when the credits had finally scrolled to the end. "He broke barriers. Just like you."

Sidney Poitier was lovely and amazing, Bubby said. As was I. And our presence in these previously all-white worlds was a gift to all those who performed and to all those who watched us.

I think that was the first time Bubby addressed the fact that I was black. On the rare occasions when she did, it was never negative. It was just one of the many things that made me so special.

I'd never felt special before. I don't think I'd ever really wanted to. That would have meant that everyone was looking at me, that I had to speak up, to risk saying the wrong thing and be judged. I preferred to hide.

But there was no disappearing at Cindy's. When we were at the dinner table, eating the meal that Patrick usually had prepared, they wanted to talk about my day, about my future. Even with Wolfie, their biological son, sitting right there, Cindy and Patrick focused their attention totally on me.

"I think my jumps are getting stronger," I'd say proudly. "I had higher extension in the *adagio* today."

"Some dancers have the right physique for dance, and others have the ability," Cindy would say as Patrick nodded approvingly. "You have both."

"You're going to be a star," Cindy said. "You're God's child."

※

WHEN I WAS STILL living with Mommy, and when she still had a car, she would sometimes pick me up from Danielle's or Reina's and we would crank up the radio and sing along to Toni Braxton.

Seven whole days, and not a word from you.

For those few minutes, it was as if we'd grabbed hands and were gliding together on a melody. But that was as close as Mommy and I ever really got. Conversation with Mommy was succinct, often superficial. Mommy was just too tired to delve deeply into my thoughts and feelings. Besides, I'm not sure that she ever developed the skills to communicate deeply when she was a child and therefore couldn't teach us. By the end of the day, after working nine to five, raising six children, and dealing with an addicted or abusive partner, she had simply run out of words.

But Cindy and I would eventually get to the point of being able to talk for long stretches of time. When she dropped me off at school, picked me up in the afternoon, and drove me home from the dance center, she asked me an endless stream of questions.

This was the first time I recall experiencing someone focused solely on me, attempting to hear what I had to say. It was terrifying for me because it was all new. I almost felt threatened and attacked.

"What are you thinking this very moment?"

"How do you feel?"

"Who is your favorite dancer?"

"What do you want to eat tonight?"

"What's so funny?"

I had no idea how to respond to her constant barrage of even these most simple questions. I started sweating. Did I even know what I was thinking or feeling? Why did she even care? It was incomprehensible that someone could have these conversations with me without critiquing my judgment and thoughts. The only times I remember Cindy showing me any anger was when she would get frustrated with my unwillingness to speak. She would not let me off the hook. She knew that being upset with me and giving me no other way out was how she would get me to open up. The Bradleys taught me to think critically, and I will forever be grateful to them for that. Still, I adjusted slowly.

Cindy would always act as though my conclusions were the wisest, most profound analyses she'd ever heard. Her approval started to pull me out of my shell. The din of life back home had made it easier, more comforting, for me to be silent, but her questions and unconditional approval bolstered me. I'd begun to hear the sound of my own voice. And I liked it.

Cindy, a white woman, also made me feel as if my blackness was the most beautiful thing in the world.

I'd always felt good about being black, despite the terrible things that Robert and his family had said about my mother and my siblings. I'd never wanted to be anything else. But to Cindy, my heritage gave me something even more exceptional.

She especially loved my full, curly hair. At home, my frizzy tresses were a bushel to be tamed. From the time I was little, my big sister Erica would blow-dry my hair, blasting away the curls and making them lie down flat. Or if I wanted to wear a ponytail, she'd pull my hair back so tight, my temples would hurt, and she'd drown every potential out-of-place strand under a glob of gel. That's just what black women did. We used flat irons and sizzling straightening combs to make our kinks bow into submission.

But Cindy liked me to wear my hair natural and free. Once, she snapped a candid shot of me walking into her room wearing a polka-dot dress she had bought me, my hair hanging loose and curly. I have to admit that at first I winced when I saw that picture. That was not the way I was taught to wear my hair, especially not in a photograph that might sit atop a mantel for years to come. But the longer I lived with the Bradleys, the more comfortable I became wearing my waves.

One day I looked at that picture and thought, *Wow, how beautiful.* It was as if I was seeing it, and myself, for the first time.

Even before I was totally at ease with it, I began to wear my hair the way that Cindy liked it more and more often. It was hard to resist her yin and yang: her soothing nature that reassured you that there was no one prettier, and the passionate spirit that roared through our household like a gale wind.

Everyone in Cindy's orbit flowed to her erratic rhythm. As the most dramatic example, she'd never asked Patrick if I could come live with them. I was just there. He may have been as mystified as Wolfie, but he never showed it and always made me feel as if his home was my home.

Cindy could also be impulsive, maybe even a little reckless.

The summer before I turned fifteen, we decided that it would be better for me to be homeschooled to allow more time for dance. There was an independent study program a few blocks from our condo. I would go there every couple of weeks to meet with a teacher, get new assignments, and be graded on the previous bundle of homework. Except for those twice-monthly appointments, Cindy no longer had to drop me off at school in the mornings. But most days she would be out the door anyway, off to run an errand, conduct business at the dance center, or set up my next performance.

So I would wake up and make breakfast for myself and Wolfie. Then I'd get him dressed, grab Misha by the leash, and together we'd walk Wolfie to his day-care center around the corner. I'd come back home, do my history or English homework, then pick up Wolfie, make him lunch, and wait for Cindy to come home to take me to the dance center in the early afternoon.

I was used to helping care for my younger siblings, so at the time my grown-up tasks didn't strike me as particularly odd, but looking back, it seems crazy that Cindy entrusted such responsibilities to me. Still, I don't think she was trying to take advantage. That was just Cindy—driven by passion, not rules. And Patrick, calm, quiet, and madly in love with his wife, let her run the show.

The perfectionist who would have me practice *pirouettes* for hours in a parking lot before a show would have to turn the house upside down searching for her misplaced keys before finally finding them still lodged in the car's ignition. Cindy would dash off to an aerobics or Pilates class, while thirteen-year-old me was left at home to take care of Wolf. Many evenings, the family would sit down to the dinner Patrick had prepared while Cindy splashed on her bangles and boots and headed to the club with her band of friends. We wouldn't see her again until morning.

CINDY WAS ALSO OBSESSED with her looks, constantly dyeing her brown locks russet red and shopping at a pace that I'd never seen. Wolfie and I spent hours outside department store dressing rooms, reading a book or playing I Spy, as Cindy tried on outfit after outfit.

"Does this make me look fat?" she'd ask again and again.

"Ummm, no," I'd dutifully respond, knowing that it would take her donning several outfits at once to add bulk to her needle-thin frame.

I actually thought it was a lot of fun, spending so much time together, sifting through the racks of beautiful things. It was especially nice that Cindy's shopping obsession included me. She loved to dress me up in pastel skirts, trendy flared jeans, and all the latest styles being worn by a fourteen-year-old girl.

I felt like Cinderella. But Mommy saw the hair, the outfits, the way I'd changed. And she didn't like it.

MOMMY CALLED ME AT Cindy's weekly to ask how things were going and tell me what was happening with my brothers and sisters. Then on weekends, I would go home to her at the motel.

We kids were pretty scattered by then. During the week, Cameron lived with his father, Robert; Lindsey often stayed with her father, Harold; and Erica continued to spend many nights at the homes of friends. Even Doug and Chris often bunked with their buddies from school. But on weekends, we would all reunite, so happy to see one another. Doug would talk about the latest outrage being done to the black man, Lindsey would crack jokes, and I would twist Cameron into some of the poses I'd learned in ballet. Our teasing and laughter drowned out the sounds of traffic on the busy streets outside.

And I now had so much to teach everyone.

Cindy wanted to make up for the years of cultural deprivation she felt I'd undergone when I'd lived with Mommy, who had so many children to take care of.

"You're going to be socializing with very important people," Cindy told me. "You need to know how to comport yourself."

So she taught me that forks went on the left and knives on the right, that there was a certain spoon for soup and another for dessert.

Cindy was also concerned about my diet and health. Before I went to live with her, I'd subsist on whatever Mommy had the budget to buy, and I'd often stuff myself with junk food that I bought in school or from motel vending machines. I loved spicy Cheetos, corn chips that were heated in the microwave and slathered with cheese squeezed out of a bottle and hot sauce.

But Cindy said that I needed to be better nourished to gain weight and strength for dancing. We had fresh vegetables every night for dinner. And with her, I tasted shrimp for the first time. After my first bite, I craved it constantly. When we went out to restaurants, I'd order shrimp scampi and a Shirley Temple every time.

So now when I went to visit Mommy, I would ask for certain things for dinner, my newly refined taste buds melding with my recently developed opinionated streak.

"Ewww," I'd say as Mommy poured canned string beans into a pot and heated them on the stove. "Why do you need to put so much salt on my mac and cheese? And none of that pepper, please!"

I'd drink water instead of the orange soda Mommy had bought. And I'd set the table before we Copelands sat down to dinner, folding the paper napkins in half and filling the mismatched glasses. I didn't want to make her feel bad, but I knew my healthy diet was contributing to a higher purpose. I needed strength to dance, and it was my responsibility to be aware of what I put in my body.

Mommy didn't appreciate my comments about food, or any of the other changes she was seeing in me. In fact, my attitude made her furious. She felt I was turning my nose up at how she'd raised me, at how she was caring for my brothers and sisters. She felt that now I thought I was better than them.

"Why didn't you comb your hair?" she asked me one Friday night after Cindy had dropped me off and I walked into the motel room.

"It *is* combed," I said defiantly. "I just didn't straighten it. I like it like this."

Mommy, frowning, sucked her teeth.

She also noticed all the new clothes.

"You're not a doll for her to dress up," she said when I pulled out a flowery jumper that I was planning to wear the day I went back to Cindy's. "And you're not her daughter. I can take you shopping."

I thought to myself, *With what money?* But I held my tongue.

After a while, I started coming home less frequently. A week would pass, then two. Cindy, to give me—as well as her dance studio—exposure, had us performing constantly, often at very high-profile gigs. Once, I danced a solo, *en pointe*, at a luncheon for the L.A. Dodgers. I had a baseball cap, a white leotard emblazoned with the Dodgers logo, and even a bat as a prop.

Another time, I—along with some of my classmates—performed at the Special Olympics. And every year we danced at Taste of San Pedro, a popular event where local restaurants set up booths on the street and offered samples of their menus to passersby.

Our primary performance home was the auditorium at San Pedro High School. But wherever we danced, our shows were usually on Saturdays or Sundays. And when I wasn't performing, I was rehearsing or taking dance classes. There was no time to go home.

That's when Mommy really started to get angry. She felt as if she was losing me completely.

My mother began calling the Bradleys more often, not to speak to me but to talk to Cindy, who would take the calls in her bedroom, beyond where I could hear. When she came back ten or twenty minutes later to wherever the rest of the family was gathered, her mouth would be stretched tight. She never shared what Mommy had said—but I could guess.

I can imagine how my mother must have felt. She probably worried that people wouldn't understand that her daughter had to move out to pursue her dancing dreams and would assume instead that she was simply a bad mother.

Our relationship was so much more complicated than that. Mommy probably envied Cindy—a woman with more resources, a supportive husband, and a comfortable home—and thought she was trying to steal her daughter away.

I don't think that was Cindy's intention. But it was true that my living with her and Patrick changed me. Before I moved in with the Bradleys, I was a thirteen-year-old girl who still played with Barbies. I hid from life in games of make-believe, in dance routines choreographed in my mother's bedroom. But when I moved out of the motel, I left my dolls behind. I was growing up.

To this day, I have no negative feelings about Cindy and Patrick. They were positive forces in my life who pushed me to become a whole person. When I had to leave them, two years after I'd moved in, it would be the most traumatic of all my departures, more wrenching than leaving Harold, more frightening than fleeing Robert. It was the hardest thing I'd ever experienced in my life.

I didn't understand it. I didn't know why I was being taken from these people who loved me so much, who had immersed me in the world of ballet, who had exposed me to art, to etiquette, to a taste of what life could and should be.

I would move from that new life to my old one, back into

a motel. And I would resent my mother so much for returning me there.

DURING MY FIRST YEAR at Cindy's school, she staged *The Nutcracker* at San Pedro High School. I danced the part of Clara, the little girl whose vivid dream of sugar plum fairies and enchanted dolls has mesmerized theatergoers for generations. Filling rows in the auditorium were Mommy and all my brothers and sisters, along with lots of our friends. It was a wonderful evening.

But when I was fourteen, a retelling of that classic story would help launch me, bringing me attention and a measure of celebrity that I had never experienced.

It was *The Chocolate Nutcracker.*

Cindy was always trying to connect me with the black dance community. Once, she found a local African American charity event that I was able to participate in. I danced a solo, *en pointe,* while a jazz saxophonist played. The great actress Angela Bassett, glowing and doe-eyed, was part of the program, and I'd gotten to meet her during the dress rehearsal. I could barely look at her, I was so excited.

I think Cindy saw *The Chocolate Nutcracker* as another chance for me to meld all my worlds, showing the classical ballet repertoire that I was mastering but also allowing me to dip into African dance and meet prominent African Americans.

The Chocolate Nutcracker was produced by the actress and choreographer Debbie Allen and added twists to the classic story of Clara and the toy soldiers come to life. Instead of Clara being taken to the land of sweets by her nutcracker-turned-prince, she'd travel the globe. And the nutcracker and his soldiers fought slithering snakes instead of militaristic mice.

My performances throughout Los Angeles were getting attention, and by then I had been the subject of several news articles talking about this late-blooming black ballerina who turned out to be a prodigy. I believe Debbie Allen had seen them and reached out to Cindy to see if I'd be interested in playing Clare, *The Chocolate Nutcracker*'s version of Clara.

Debbie was warm but no-nonsense. At first, she had me work privately with her choreographers to make sure I was capable of all it took to be the lead in the ballet. After I'd won the part, they actually wound up having to alter the dance sequences to make them more challenging for me. I have video footage of my rehearsing for hours and hours.

Since Clare would be traveling to other countries in the ballet's world, like Egypt, part of my preparation included taking classes with Debbie to learn various ethnic dance forms. Cindy drove me to Debbie's studio in Los Angeles, and it was a world apart from what I was used to. There were all these beautiful black boys and girls engaged in African and Brazilian dance. There were live drummers, pounding out a beat, and me, in the middle of it all, in my pointe shoes.

We performed at UCLA's Royce Hall, and I got to share the stage and dialogue with Debbie, who played Clare's aunt. I was fine doing African dance one minute, and dancing *en pointe* the next. But holding a mic and talking to Debbie Allen? *That* was scary.

But becoming Clare was wonderful. I again felt that sass coming out of me, the way it had in the Point Fermin Elementary talent show, or the way it did at that first performance Cindy set up at a park in San Pedro. The way it did every time I was on a stage, before a crowd.

I remember the audience giving me a standing ovation. And Mommy, there, sitting close to the front row, gave me the most love of all. She was hooting and hollering on her feet, clapping like it was the greatest performance she'd ever seen. It's not exactly what you would hear at the Metropolitan Opera House where ABT performs, but it was loving and genuine. It just made me want to do it all again.

Later, Debbie Allen would tell the *Los Angeles Times Magazine* that I was "a child who dances in her soul . . . I can't imagine her doing anything else."

After that performance, I was on fire.

More articles about my talent followed, in the *Daily Breeze*, San Pedro's local paper, as well as other news outlets. People were calling Cindy's dance studio wanting to know when and where this phenomenal little girl they'd heard so much about would be performing next.

My school identity morphed as well. I'd always been Doug and Erica and Chris's little sister who happened to be captain of the drill team. Now I was *the ballerina.*

As shy as I was, all the attention could be a little overwhelming, and I felt uncomfortable at first. But the glare was somehow easier to absorb because it was connected to ballet, my new love. It was like I was carrying the audience with me for a little while after I'd left the stage.

I had been dancing for well over a year and decided to give up the drill team. I wanted to focus every hour that I could, every bit of my energy and creativity on ballet.

After *The Chocolate Nutcracker*, Cindy decided it was time for me to perform my dream role for the first time. The San Pedro Dance Center would stage *Don Quixote*, and I would be Kitri.

With so many performances under my belt, Cindy also said it was time for me to enter competitions, to go up against other experienced ballerinas and win broader recognition for my talent.

My first competition would be one of the most difficult and prestigious, the Music Center's Spotlight Awards. The competition, which has been staged annually for more than two decades, gives out tens of thousands of dollars in scholarships to teenagers who excel in the arts. There were prizes in various categories, including ballet, modern dance, jazz, and classical music performance. And the judges were at the pinnacle of those genres. Those who won have gone on to perform with the Metropolitan Opera and Alvin Ailey, among other premier cultural institutions.

Since I was preparing to play Kitri in the dance center's production of *Don Quixote*, we thought it made sense for me to perform a variation from that same ballet at the Spotlight Awards.

But it was a daunting selection, a complicated, arduous dance sequence that most dancers would not have dared to attempt with barely two years of training. And they certainly wouldn't have debuted it on the Los Angeles Music Center's grand stage, in front of some of the giants of the ballet world.

I would also be preparing in the glare of the television spotlight on KCET, a local TV station. The program was called

Beating the Odds and it was doing a segment on some of the teens competing in the Spotlight Awards. They knew of me from all the articles that had been written, and when the show's producers learned I was one of the entrants, they picked me as one of the handful of teens they would follow.

I was one of two dancers whom they trailed. The crew was there when I auditioned and at some of my rehearsals, and crew members even spent some time at home with me at the Bradleys.

To prepare for the Spotlight Awards, I practiced six days a week for a month. The variation I would perform was Kitri's third act solo, and I would have to execute the famous thirty-two *fouettés* at the end of the variation.

I should say now that when I danced, I was never nervous, not during rehearsal, not during a performance. It was as if I went into a trance.

Ballet studio walls are lined with mirrors, and you are supposed to use them to correct yourself, to adjust your body or extend your legs to reflect your teacher's direction about how to improve. But to this day, while there are times when I pay attention to what I see in the mirrors, to master new steps, more often it's as if they're not even there. My visual memory, my physical intuition, takes over.

I think I've always danced beyond the mirror, transcending the tedium and bounding right to the joy.

That's what you need to stand out on the stage. Many dancers have a body that's capable, that has the facility to perform, but they get onstage and they don't have "it," that blissful spark that makes it impossible for the audience members to get the performance out of their heads. For me, even in the classroom, it was always showtime.

When I was seventeen, I went to New York to participate in ABT's summer program. Lupe Serrano, a woman whom I still love, was one of my first teachers. She had been a prima ballerina in her day and was now a ballet mistress.

After I executed various combinations, she walked over to me, disapproval creasing her brow.

"Why are you giving so much at the barre?" she asked me with exasperation. "This isn't a performance!"

"Oh," I said, surprised and more than a little embarrassed. "I'm sorry."

In ballet, every step has a million moving parts. Your head must be in the right position, your body in alignment, your feet turned just so. It requires precision to get it all right. But for me, ballet has always been more than a technical matrix. It's fun.

Cindy had an incredible ability to really showcase the music in her movement. She was both an actress and a dancer. I emulated it because it was all I knew. Her arms, her *épaulement*, her elegant and feminine style, definitely rubbed off on me. That became my approach when I danced. Though this was not the way most schools taught you to approach ballet—prioritizing a basic understanding of your placement, lines, and strength— my training at the San Pedro Dance Center was based on movement, music, and performance. Very few develop these qualities, even after a lifetime of training. I had it from day one. In preparation for Kitri, I studied Gelsey and Paloma endlessly. I paid close attention to the way their heads moved, the way their elbows were always in a forward position ahead of their wrists when their hands were on their hips. Kitri was strong and in control. I understood it all!

Cindy said to me during one of my rehearsals for the

grand *pas de deux* in the third act, with Charles Maple, "How do you know when to lift your chin? I never told you." She was stumped. I didn't really have an answer. The accent in the music came and with it so did the lift of my chin to match. I never questioned or quite understood how: I just knew. It was my instinct, and the marvelous thing was that it was usually right.

Not a performance? Of course it was. Always.

BUT WHEN I WAS fifteen, in the final days before the Spotlight Awards, I began to stumble. I was having trouble completing my full series of turns. The morning of the competition, I felt something I'd never experienced before a performance: nerves.

It was a feeling that was so new in connection with dance that at first I didn't even know what it was. I suppose the difference this time was that I'd never felt so pressured before when it came to ballet. There were thousands of dollars on the line, and an entire city watching me.

Cindy had begun to worry during my final practices. Then, the morning of the performance, during the dress rehearsal at the Dorothy Chandler Pavilion, she seemed almost frantic.

I couldn't get through the *fouettés*. It's a classic bravura move that is one of the prima ballerina's staples. You're supposed to keep going and going and going, through thirty-two exhausting turns, and I couldn't complete them. I was probably just exhausted, but seeing the way Cindy reacted—the tension and fear on her face—panicked me.

"You have to get this," she said nervously. "This is your big chance. Gerald Arpino will be there."

Gerald Arpino was the artistic director and cofounder of the Joffrey Ballet, one of the world's top dance companies. He would be one of the judges.

We only had fifteen minutes to practice, and then we had to get off the stage and give the next competitor a chance to rehearse. I was freaked out, and Cindy saw it.

Then Cindy had an idea.

She hurriedly took me down into the underground garage where her car was parked. She opened all the car doors to create a makeshift screen, then stuck a cassette of the music I would dance to in the car's player. She calmed me, reassuring me that even though I had a decade less training than my competitor, I had something she didn't: a sparkle, a will from within that wasn't about the number of *fouettés* I did, or how high I kicked my leg, but the passion and potential the judges would see in me.

Right there, she rechoreographed my variation.

Instead of thirty-two turns, I would do sixteen. And then I would go into a *piqué ménage*, a circular traveling step, to finish out the music.

It was a backup plan, which I embraced gratefully. Cindy cranked up Kitri's music, and we got to work. Instead of in my pointe shoes, I learned and rehearsed the new routine in my sneakers.

That taught me something. When I'm on the stage, I always want to appear clean, and strong, never out of control. That is what it means to be a professional. And that day, at the Spotlight Awards, I learned you should always have a backup plan, so you can always deliver a performance that is sharp and refined. Even if your body fails, your performance never will.

There are dancers who believe that you won't try as hard if you know there's a safety net. But I don't agree.

My life in the ballet studio is devoted to the goal of perfecting the impossibly precise and rarefied steps of a centuries-old technique. You teach your body to depend on its muscle memory with repetition of the steps in rehearsal so that when you are onstage and are presented with the unpredictable elements of the theater you can still thrive.

Onstage, the lights change your balance and focus and warm the air enough to soften stiff pointe shoes. A costume adds weight and restrictions to a dancer's movement. The live orchestra and often temperamental conductor challenge you to now think on your toes if there is a sudden change in tempo. And then there's your own excitement, the rush that comes with a live performance. Often, instincts tempt you to react in opposition to the choreography your body knows so well.

And with all these outside and internal pressures, dancers are still expected to meet the standards of classical "perfection." I've had to create my own standard. As a professional (and a perfectionist), my goal is to be consistent in giving an exciting, emotionally charged, and technically sound performance. The rehearsal studio is the time where I take risky chances and fall on my face so I can learn where to rein it in. I would never take those risks on the stage in front of a hungry audience. They deserve better.

Some dancers feel different, taking gambles onstage in pursuit of that chance that a risk will pay off and create a once-in-a-lifetime performance. I guess that's why live theater is so exciting.

But that day, at the Spotlight Awards, I learned to be prepared and focus on what's important.

It was finally showtime. I took the stage, dressed in a red tutu edged with golden lace that Cindy had made just for the competition.

Mommy, Lindsey, Cindy, and Bubby were all there. The theater was dark despite the white spotlights. I felt cool and determined, even as I congratulated the performer who finished just before my entrance.

I went to my backup routine and performed it flawlessly. Up and down on my toes, twirling across the stage, brandishing a ruby-red fan that I flung aside before I began my turns. I became Kitri, fire in my eyes, flirting fiercely as though I were batting my eyes at every last audience member. As I finished my performance, I threw my arm into the air with my head thrown back, a smile nearly splitting my face, and one hand cocked saucily on my hip. I had danced—happy, free.

Then it was over. I was relieved and joyful.

"I got through all my *fouettés!*" I said to the program producers standing backstage. "I'm really happy."

From there it's all a blur. I won the top prize—five thousand dollars—for ballet. I have the trophy in my apartment to this very day.

Then, after the other winners were announced, we all gathered backstage.

It was bedlam.

Gerald Arpino ran up to me. He grabbed me and wouldn't let me go.

"You're my baby, you're my baby," he said, hugging me tightly. "You have to come dance with me! You have to come to the Joffrey!"

There were camera flashes galore, and the KCET film crew was there, too. A photograph of Mr. Arpino hugging me appeared on the cover of a local TV guide the week that the *Beating the Odds* anniversary special aired, as well as in several newspapers. It was a huge deal, Gerald Arpino's embracing me, wanting me.

I began to see the vista to a world beyond what I had ever previously imagined.

✀

WITH A BURST OF confidence from winning the competition, I began to go on auditions for the summer programs offered by the most prestigious ballet companies.

Cindy felt it was important for me to audition for as many as possible, both to gain the experience of being in intense situations around elite dancers and for these various companies to get a look at me, in the hope that I could join them one day.

After the Spotlight Awards, I was offered spots by the Joffrey and ABT, whose Summer Intensive director, Rebecca Wright, had also been a judge. But I still had to audition for both in order for them to determine how large my scholarship would be.

I also tried out for the summer programs offered by Dance Theatre of Harlem, Pacific Northwest Ballet, and San Francisco Ballet.

In the subjective hierarchy of the ballet world, ABT reigns supreme and is known as America's National Company. You have to go overseas to find its peers—the Paris Opera, Royal Ballet, Bolshoi Ballet, the Kirov Ballet, La Scala, English National Ballet, the Royal Danish Ballet, and the Stuttgart Ballet.

Back in North America, the New York City Ballet follows close behind ABT in prestige, though it stands a bit apart as its company primarily dances the distinctive works created by its founder, George Balanchine, rather than a traditional, classical repertoire. Next comes San Francisco Ballet, followed by the National Ballet of Canada, Boston Ballet, Pacific Northwest Ballet, the Joffrey, and the ballet companies of Miami and Houston.

I received offers from all the ballet companies I auditioned for, except for one: the New York City Ballet. Every single company awarded me a scholarship. The New York City Ballet didn't even want me to attend. This news was extremely confusing to me. Cindy has praised my "Balanchinesque" physique as the ideal figure for a ballerina to possess. We thought I'd be perfect for its vision and distinctive style. I showed up for the audition in a pale pink leotard and pink tights. With my hair pulled into a bun on the top of my head, I even looked like that music box ballerina image that every girl envisioned.

Or so I thought.

Ballet summer intensive programs are moneymakers. If you have the body and can pay the fees, you generally have an automatic in. Then, once you get there, talent and ability is what determines if you will be asked to stay year-round and train at the school.

So, when I got their rejection letter, Cindy's analysis was stark. They didn't want me because I was black.

That was the note she made me keep, and I dutifully tucked it in a photo album.

The others did want me, though—San Francisco Ballet, perhaps, most of all. The director called Cindy to tell her how thrilled they would be to have me. They also offered the most generous package—not only tuition, but room and board and my airfare to fly up the coast.

I also liked the idea that, compared to the others, it was closer to home. It would be the first time that I would be going so far away.

So I chose them.

A few weeks later, I was off to San Francisco.

Chapter 5

SUMMER IN SAN FRANCISCO is an oxymoron.

I arrived in June, but it was so cold that I had to buy bulky gray sweatshirts with the city's name on them to keep warm. I might as well have scrawled TOURIST on my forehead with a Magic Marker. But I didn't care. Wearing the dorky garments was still better than freezing. My face stayed moist from the gauzelike fog that was thick enough to skim off the bay. It swaddled the city through the night and skittered off in the morning with the sun.

I was fifteen years old and nervous about leaving home on my own. I'd been on a plane only once before, the previous year, when I'd flown to South Dakota to be a guest dancer in a production of *The Nutcracker.*

Charles Maple, my erstwhile partner at Cindy's studio and former soloist with my dream company, ABT, had invited *me* to dance with him in a revised production of *The Nutcracker.* I was ecstatic! My first traveling dance gig, at fifteen years old, was a major accomplishment, though I have to admit I was most excited about flying for the first time. I had worked for months with Charles, learning his choreography. When we arrived in South Dakota, which was about as foreign to me as Beijing or Genoa would later be, we entered a studio filled with maybe a hundred young girls, all of them white. This was not unusual for me. I was ready to work. The girls and their parents had odd looks on their faces. I didn't know why.

Charles pulled me aside. "Don't be alarmed," he whispered, "but I need you to act as though you are trying out for the lead part of Clara along with the other girls in this room." I was very confused . . . and a little hurt. Why was I here, if not to dance the part I'd practiced? Charles taught the choreography and the dancers followed. I pretended to be learning it for the first time.

After a long grueling "audition" day, Charles and I headed to dinner. He explained to me that though he knew how gifted I was, and how perfect I'd be to portray Clara the way he intended, he had to bring me here to show them how great I was in the flesh. Otherwise, they'd never be able to see past my skin color. I played the part of Clara in two performances in South Dakota. By the end of the day, it'd been clear to even the most competitive dancers and parents that I deserved the role. Everyone was warm, friendly, and complimentary of my talent.

I learned maybe a decade later that Charles was extremely fearful about that trip. He took a big risk in bringing a black girl into what could have potentially been a very racist environment. Today, I think the risk was well worth it. Showing people—who may not even have been aware of their subtle prejudices or doubts, that I was just as capable as them because of the color of my skin—that they were wrong was more powerful than any minor discomfort I might have felt.

But that was just a few days. My stay in San Francisco would last six weeks.

Cindy's friend Kate accompanied me on the one-hour flight up the coast. But she flew right back to Los Angeles after dropping me off at the University of San Francisco dormitory, where San Francisco Ballet summer intensive students were housed.

Pulling my gray suitcase behind me, I found a handwritten sign on my dorm room's door: I'M KAYAKO, it read. KINDA QUIET AND SHY UNTIL I GET TO KNOW YOU.

I felt relieved. That sounded just like me.

Kayako would be my roommate for the summer, and she truly was like me in many ways. She was part black and part Japanese, and she had grown up in Lakewood, Washington, a small town near Tacoma. I felt as if we had been placed together on purpose. How often do you find a black girl in ballet? But whether our pairing had been by design or the result of fate, I was glad to see her. She would become one of my dearest friends.

Kayako was a lot taller than me, and a little bit lighter in complexion, with skin that was more like cream than cocoa. And she had a beautiful mane of wild, curly jet-black hair.

The next day, grabbing breakfast in the dormitory cafeteria, we met the girl who would become our other confidante, Jessica. She was Asian American and also towered over me, probably by a foot. But while she looked years older, she had a goofy sense of humor, and we'd sit around cracking one another up with corny jokes while munching on Snickers bars. I would become even closer to her than I was to Kayako.

The three of us would hang out, exploring San Francisco whenever we weren't in the ballet studio. We went to the arcades on Pier 39, pitching balls through hoops to win stuffed animals and nibbling cotton candy and Dippin' Dots.

We took the bus out to Great America Amusement Park and rode roller coasters with names like the FireFall. We went to the movies and saw *I Still Know What You Did Last Summer*, sifted through tights and leotards at the Capezio dance store, and window-shopped in Union Square, gazing at high-priced outfits that we could never afford.

Though all three of us were close, Kayako seemed more mature than Jessica and me. Unlike me, she had a boyfriend right away, a boy who was also a student in the summer intensive program; I was still too awkward for even a childish summer romance. I remember often leaving our room so the two of them could make out. I'd wander over to Jessica's or down to the common area and watch TV.

While we spent just about all of our free time together, I didn't see Jessica or Kayako much during the day. I didn't have any classes with them. Despite my limited training, I had been placed in the highest levels of the summer program, with the most advanced students. Lola de Ávila, the school's associate director, insisted on it.

In any ballet program, incoming students have to take a class that will allow the staff to determine where the students should be placed. Quickly figuring out the right spots for dozens of students is a daunting task.

The first things teachers focus on are your body and the quality of your movement. With my long, thin legs that sloped backward and my supersize feet, I had the ideal body for ballet.

And my movement—fluid, fearless—came naturally. Seeing that, the teachers that summer—and in summers to come—felt that I belonged in classes with those who were the most experienced. There hadn't been enough time for them to assess my true strengths and weaknesses, but they understood that what I did know, I could articulate with precision.

Summer intensive programs are also a critical rung on the ladder for young dancers aspiring to one day be a part of American Ballet Theatre, the Joffrey, or any of the other prestigious ballet companies in the United States. At the end of a program, the artistic staff usually selects a handful of the best-performing students and invites them to attend their school year-round, with the hope that they will one day be good enough to join the actual company.

I think that before I had taken my first class, Lola de Ávila and the artistic director of San Francisco Ballet had decided that they intended to offer me a year-round spot. That would explain why they had been so generous, offering me a full scholarship to their summer program that covered not only my tuition, housing, and equipment, but even my flights to and from San Francisco. A slot in their school was mine for the taking.

My reputation as a prodigy had preceded me. But despite my gifts, the reality was that there were huge holes in my knowledge of ballet. I had started so late, and was so green, that there were many terms, steps, and even productions that I had never heard of.

It was clear that I had much to learn from the first day I walked into a class. The other students—most of them white, some of them Asian, and from Russia, Japan, and Spain, as well as from cities and small towns throughout the States—had been dancing their entire lives. And it showed.

We took classes on *pas de deux* and variations, in which you took a solo from a well-known ballet and learned a particular interpretation. The other dancers had performed the variations that we learned many times, but I hadn't danced most of them even once.

The first ballet that we studied was *Sleeping Beauty*. Of course I'd heard of the classic fairy tale, in which Princess Aurora, cursed by an evil fairy, is doomed to prick her finger and die on her sixteenth birthday. She is rescued by the Lilac Fairy, who counters the spell with one of her own to ensure that Aurora only falls asleep. Princess Aurora is ultimately revived by a prince's sweet kiss.

But I didn't know Tchaikovsky's balletic retelling, the slow rhythm of its *adagio*, the broad, bounding leaps of its *grands jetés*. I'd never seen the ballet before and wasn't familiar with any of the choreography.

I also quickly found out that summer that I lacked stamina. I wasn't used to being on my feet, dancing in pointe shoes, for hours each day, and my body ached from the rigor. By the time we were done with our classes in the late afternoon, my feet would be red and swollen. I'd hobble back to the dorm, barely able to walk, let alone do one more *plié*. Jessica would meet Kayoko and me at our room, and we'd fill small trash cans with ice and water. Then we'd plunge our exhausted feet into the chill.

But the teachers embraced me, pushed me, nurtured me— Lola de Ávila most of all.

San Pedro had a large Latino population, and many of my friends and schoolmates had parents or grandparents who had immigrated to California from Mexico or Central America. But I had never met a Spaniard before. I assumed Lola, trained in Zaragoza, Spain, would look like my neighbors back home: brown-skinned and raven-haired. But she didn't look that way at all.

Lola was very pale, with aquiline features and a short brown pouf of hair. She was petite and spoke with a beautiful, lilting accent.

She had originally been taught to dance by her mother, María de Ávila. She went on to perform in *La Sylphide, Giselle,* and *Raymonda;* to partner with Rudolf Nureyev; and to teach at the National Ballet of Spain.

After I was offered, and accepted, the scholarship by San Francisco Ballet Company, Lola called to speak to Cindy and me. She told us how happy she and the other directors were that I was coming and told us what I should expect when I arrived. Those were the types of details that most schools would simply put in a letter. It was rare, flattering, and comforting that the associate director would take the time to call and relay that information personally.

That's the way Lola would be throughout the entire summer, constantly hugging, holding, and guiding me. She was a wonderful teacher, always accepting of where I was in terms of what I knew and didn't know, taking the time to explain it all and giving me the time to absorb it.

PETIT ALLEGRO DESCRIBES A series of small jumps and quick footwork. It differs from the *grand allegro*, where the leaps are high and your legs are extended fully. There are many ways to execute it, from the very basic to a combination of intricate steps. But basic or advanced, there were many steps I hadn't learned and was now seeing for the first time.

In my classes, I usually followed along by watching and imitating the other, more experienced students, not really knowing the steps that I was doing but able to do well enough. Yet in class when we did *petit allegro*, I was just lost. Finally, I moved to the side and stood alone because I couldn't keep up. For the first time, my abilities failed me.

That's when Lola walked over, gently grabbed me by the hand, and led me to the front of the class.

We stood together.

"That is a *brisé*," she whispered in my ear, describing the rapid swishing of one leg in front of the other as you leap to the side, breaking down the *petit allegro* into tiny bits so I could grasp it, master it.

"This is a *temps de cuisse*," she said, describing the motion, placing one foot in front of the other, then jumping with both feet before landing on one.

As shy as I was, I normally would have been mortified at being led to the front of the class, without a chance to practice first, unsure of the lesson being taught. But the ingenue who had cringed when Cindy stood her in front of the group at the Boys and Girls Club to stretch and shape her limbs had vanished. As Lola whispered in my ear—"*soubresaut*," "*échappé sauté*"—I felt exhilarated, as if I was cracking the code that would lead me to a wonderful treasure. I listened and watched, learned and echoed.

About two weeks after the start of the program, I began to have occasional private meetings with Lola in her office. It was too early for the company to issue an official invitation, but I think she wanted me to start thinking about what it would be like to stay and study with the school for the entire year. It was an actual school where all the young dancers took classes in English, history, science, and mathematics, but our academics would be bookended by ballet. There would be *fouettés* and formulas, *relevés* and similes.

Lola was not the only instructor who took a particular interest in me. My *pas de deux* teacher would use me as his model for the class, much as Charles had done, lifting, holding, and turning me in front of the other dancers.

"You see," he would yell in his baritone, holding me aloft with one arm as I stretched my body like an arrow. "This is what a classical line looks like. Extend! Balance!"

In ballet, appearance is critical. That may seem superficial or frivolous, but in an art form that is visual, and so much about grace and suppleness, it definitely matters.

You can have everything that is required physically for ballet, the capability to execute each step perfectly, but if your head is not proportional to the rest of your body, or your eyes are too close together, it could mean the difference between acceptance and rejection by a premier ballet company. Things that may not matter in the studio show glaringly onstage as the corps de ballet performs the garden scene in *Le Corsaire*.

It takes so many things to be a great ballerina: talent, strength, the ability to pick up choreography and then turn on an inner light when you perform. Having the right combination is the difference between being an artist who can capture the nuances of light in a watercolor and one who paints by number. I don't think that most people realize that.

I had a tiny head, a long neck, boatlike feet, a compact torso—an appearance that would be imperfect by most conventional standards of beauty. But on a stage, floating through the make-believe village in *Giselle*, or the provincial court of *Raymonda*, I was ideal.

A time would come, sooner than I realized, when I would be told that I was too heavy, that my breasts were too big, that my skin was too dark.

But Cindy had always reminded me that when Balanchine described the storybook ballerina, he was talking about me. That I was perfect. And in those golden summers before I hit puberty, in the eyes of the ballet world, I was.

∽

WHEN LOLA SHOWED ME extra attention, the other girls in the program didn't seem to mind. I was such a beginner, and most were so far ahead of me in knowledge and practice, that I don't think they saw me as competition.

There were roughly two hundred students in the summer program, including perhaps eighty boys. Many of us hung out with one another, eating breakfast, lunch, and dinner together, and occasionally forming a rowdy caravan that wended through the streets of San Francisco, reveling in our temporary freedom from home and ballet.

But there were a few girls who clung to one another and kept their distance. They weren't mean, just in a world unto themselves. Back in San Pedro, I had never been one of the popular, cool kids, and those girls existed even in ballet, all cliquish, glossy, and gossipy.

They seemed more mature than me and my friends, talking about boys and all the summer intensives they'd been to, conversations I had nothing to contribute to. And they would party on the weekends, staying up all night, drinking beer and wine coolers they got some older boys to buy. Meanwhile, my friends and I would order pizza, tell silly jokes, and be in bed by eleven.

For all of us, though, Alanis Morisette's album *Jagged Little Pill* was the sound track of the summer.

And isn't it ironic

Don't you think?

I spoke to Mommy and Cindy several times a week, telling them about the friends I'd made, the new things I was learning. Over the Fourth of July weekend, Mommy came to visit and brought all my brothers and sisters.

For some reason, though they had long been separated and continued to have a tense relationship, Robert came, too. Looking back, I assume it was because Cameron was going on a road trip and Robert wanted to be there to look after him. Besides, Robert and I had always gotten along, at least better than he had with my siblings. They drove up on a Friday, and we spent the weekend visiting Fisherman's Wharf and Haight-Ashbury. Cameron, who was only about eight years old, stopped at one point to play chess with an older gentleman downtown. He was pensive and brilliant.

On Sunday, before they made the six-hour drive back to San Pedro, we stopped at an International House of Pancakes for breakfast.

"You know," Mommy said, irritation clouding her voice,

"the school's director was surprised that I was in your life. They thought Cindy was your sole guardian."

I nodded, focusing on my scrambled eggs.

She continued. "I saw Jackie and her mother the other day." Jackie, my best friend from middle school, and I hadn't seen each other very much after I began to be homeschooled and became consumed with my dance classes. "They were so excited about your getting accepted into the program up here. They said they wanted to hear all about it when you got back."

She took a sip of her orange juice. "You know, Misty, we all miss you," she continued. "I think when this summer is over, we need to start thinking about you coming back home to live with me."

I nodded. Not because I agreed, but because I didn't want to talk about it. I was desperate to end the conversation before it got started. I took a bite of my toast, though it was dry and tasteless in my mouth.

The next three weeks flew by, and sooner than I wanted it to be, the program was over. On the last day, I was summoned to a meeting in Lola's office.

She was there, perched in front of her wooden shelves lined with books and photographs. Sitting beside her was Helgi Tómasson, San Francisco Ballet's artistic director.

Lola spoke first.

"You know how impressed we are with you, Misty," she said softly. "We think you have the potential to be a great dancer, but you need consistent training to refine your technique. We would like you to come to our school and study with us for the full year."

Helgi sat silently beside her. I'd seen him only a few times, when he would enter the studio and watch the students dance.

He never stayed more than a few minutes, and I'd never heard his voice. Until now. "If you keep working hard," he said, "I can see you one day being a part of our company."

The invitation wasn't unexpected, but still I was overwhelmed and flattered. I managed to eke out a thank-you and told them I would talk about it with my mother and teacher back home.

I floated out of the office, buoyed by their belief in me. Back in the studio, I began stretching before class, as usual. That's when I noticed the whispered chatter.

All the girls knew that I had been summoned to Lola's office—and what that meant. Only two other girls and a couple boys in the entire program had received similar invitations.

One girl, speaking in a voice loud enough to carry, decided to express what so many of the others had been murmuring.

"Why'd they ask *her* to stay?" she asked. "She doesn't have enough training. Anyone could see that."

I continued stretching but could feel heat rising in my cheeks. I was embarrassed, and the self-doubt that plagued me in so many areas of my life—but so rarely when it came to dance—crept back into my mind.

Do I really deserve this? I asked myself. *So many of these other girls are so much more experienced, so much stronger. Why me?*

I wanted to run away, to retreat to my dorm room, lock the door, and privately dance my sadness away, just the way I did when I was younger, back home. But the day was only beginning. I still had to get through my ballet classes, dancing beside those same girls who had been jealously grumbling behind my back. I couldn't flee. I had to block out the criticism, the pain, and stand my ground.

At the end of the day, we took a class picture. I felt uncomfortable, but I found my place, in the center of it all, and smiled bravely.

❦

WHAT MADE ME FEEL even worse is that I knew that some of those girls who'd expected to be asked to stay had set their sights on one day dancing professionally with San Francisco Ballet Company. And I knew even before it was officially offered that I wouldn't be accepting a full-year scholarship from the school. I didn't even plan on returning to San Francisco Ballet's intensive program the following summer.

It really hadn't been up to me. Mommy had told me several times that she couldn't wait for me to be back in Southern California, and while Cindy had expected me to get an invitation from the San Francisco Ballet School, she had told me in many of our phone conversations that I needed more training back home with her. She didn't believe that I would get the same attention in a big ballet school and that my technique would suffer if I didn't have time to clean up and hone all the little details of my dancing.

Though I knew San Francisco Ballet Company was one of the best in the country, if not the world, and I loved the care and warmth Lola and the many teachers had shown me, I was okay with the decision Cindy and my mother had made. The ultimate prize for me had always been ABT.

At the very start of the summer program in San Francisco, Jessica and I had decided we were both going to be in ABT's summer intensive the following year. "See you there," we both wrote in our farewell notes, scribbled in each other's photo albums.

ABT had been my goal since I first saw its dancers on the TV in Cindy and Patrick's home, since I'd seen Paloma Herrera dance the role of Kitri in *Don Quixote* at the Dorothy Chandler Pavilion in Los Angeles. And being in ABT's summer intensive was a stepping-stone to one day being a part of that professional company.

The last night of our summer in San Francisco, all the girls gathered in a common room reserved just for us. We had pizza and listened to Alanis Morissette together one final time. We stayed up all night, and Jessica handed me a note saying that whenever she saw cotton candy or took a bite out of a piece of rock candy, she would think of me.

I was sad to leave. My first taste of independence had been sweet. I'd forged connections with a lot of the girls, made many new friends. And I'd grown so much as a dancer, with my training far surpassing what I'd received in San Pedro.

I also knew there were issues starting to break out back home between Mommy and Cindy. Mommy's entreaties for me to come home to her had become more urgent each passing week. Cindy also was becoming more insistent, telling me how much I needed her guidance and care to help prepare me for the career looming before me.

That was the tension I was returning to.

When my plane landed at Los Angeles International Airport the next afternoon, Cindy was there, waiting.

I hopped into her car and made her play my Alanis Morisette CD all the way home.

Chapter 6

❧

ON THE WEEKENDS, WHEN I'd return home to the Sunset Inn and Mommy from Cindy's, I began to hear a word mentioned again and again.

Brainwashed.

"Come on, Misty!" Doug and Chris would yell in unison. "The popcorn's ready and the game's on."

My brothers knew I'd never particularly liked sports. "No thanks," I'd say, clutching a copy of *Pointe* magazine. "I'm going to go into Mommy's room and read."

"Ummm," Doug would say, smirking and giving Chris a knowing glance, "you can't take a break from ballet for a minute? That woman's got you *brainwashed.*"

Or there was the time Chris had made a pot of spaghetti with meat sauce. He'd used ground beef. I preferred turkey.

Erica looked at me and frowned. "You didn't complain about ground beef before," she said, clearly irritated. "Would you prefer caviar? Cindy's got you living in a dream world.

"But I guess you should be able to eat what you want at *her* house," Erica added, sharpening the blade for the final dig. "After all, with all that publicity you bring her dinky school, you're probably paying for it."

I'd mostly ignore my family's snarky comments. Ribbing and teasing had always been a big part of our family chatter. But it was becoming clear that there was a lot of talk about me behind my back that was happening during the week, while I stayed at Cindy's.

I knew Mommy felt that I was starting to put on airs when I came home, not wanting the food that she bought, turning up my nose at the crowded motel room where we lived. I think she was telling my brothers and sisters that Cindy was trying to make me feel that I was better than them.

My brothers and sisters and I were still extremely close and fiercely protective of one another. They would boast to their friends about the scholarships I'd been offered, the places where I'd been performing. They came to every show that they could, and no one, except maybe Mommy, ever cheered louder.

But their resentment of Cindy was building. I don't think they were jealous of my new life. I think that they were worried that I might be being used or exploited, and they were concerned what my living apart from them—with a woman they felt didn't respect our mother or them—was doing to our family.

Of course I disagreed. I knew what the term *brainwashed* meant, and my life with Cindy and Patrick had been the furthest thing from it. Still, it was true that I brought a whirlwind of publicity to Cindy's studio and school, with all the accolades I received and the news coverage about me.

Cindy readily acknowledged that I was her star. She would sometimes sell as many as two thousand tickets to one of her school's performances, the audience packed with balletomanes and the curious, all of whom had come to see the ballet prodigy who'd been discovered at the Boys and Girls Club and bloomed in a working-class corner of San Pedro.

But I still think all that was a happy, unintentional outcome, not the goal. The Bradleys had helped unearth and hone my gift. Instead of treating me like a student or project, they embraced me as a daughter. I was still shy, but thanks to their nurturing, I now knew that my voice was worth hearing.

And as much as I loved my family, I hadn't missed the chaos or the day-to-day uncertainty that we'd lived with. I liked having my own room, even one that I shared with a little boy. I loved coming home to the smells of the peach cobbler and lemon pie that Patrick had baked. I cherished not having to worry about whether I would eat or where I would sleep. I appreciated that the only thing I had to do was be a girl who loved to dance.

But my brothers and sisters didn't understand. They were all on Mommy's side.

I RETURNED FROM SAN FRANCISCO a different ballerina from when I left, much more educated and refined.

One of the many new steps I'd learned over the summer was a *temps de cuisse,* something I had never heard of, let alone attempted, before.

During one of my first classes back at the San Pedro Dance Center, I did the step literally without missing a beat. Cindy was in awe. She called Patrick, then asked me to do it over and over and over again, displaying what I had learned.

When I glided across the floor, my *glissades* were smoother. When I did a *grand jeté*, I leaped higher, extended farther. When I performed an *entrechat*, jumping in the air, crisscrossing my feet the way a bird flaps its wings, I felt like a fairy suspended in the sky. Cindy was elated.

I was, too. But I also began to feel a bit as if I'd outgrown Cindy, her studio, and her teaching—if not her devotion.

Meanwhile, my conversations with Mommy were growing more and more fraught.

"What they're doing isn't right," she'd yell when she called me on the phone during the week. "They're trying to take you away from me. I'm your mother! You have a family! You don't need them."

"They're not trying to take me away!" I'd yell back. "They've done nothing but help me!"

It seemed every time we spoke those first couple of weeks after I returned from San Francisco, Mommy and I were performing a variation of our own tortured ballet. Mommy would yell that the Bradleys were up to no good and turning me against her; I would scream in their defense and then, feeling torn and exasperated, I'd hang up the phone and run to my room, in tears.

Finally, one weekend when I was at the motel with Mommy, the moment I'd been dreading arrived.

"You're moving back home," she said with finality.

It made sense, she explained. The fact that San Francisco Ballet had offered me a full scholarship for the summer, and then the chance to be a year-round student, showed that I didn't need Cindy anymore: I was good enough, and had learned enough, to get major opportunities on my own. Besides, Mommy added, I had probably learned more during those six weeks in San Francisco than Cindy could ever teach me.

I would also be going back to San Pedro High School. Mommy had already called the Board of Education to make sure the school knew that I would be re-enrolling.

Mommy had thought of everything. She'd even made plans for me to continue dancing. Elizabeth Cantine, the drill-team instructor who had first encouraged me to take Cindy's ballet class and then paid for my leotards and pointe shoes when I went to Cindy's studio, had become as much a part of my mother's life as mine. As the relationship between Mommy and Cindy deteriorated, Mommy starting calling on Liz, who became a go-between for the two, expressing each one's feelings and concerns to the other, trying to calm the building storm.

When Mommy had made up her mind that I would return home, she enlisted Liz to help find a new ballet school that I could attend in the afternoons or on weekends. I would begin training at the Lauridsen Ballet Centre, a small dance school in Torrance, immediately.

Mommy had it all figured out, but I wouldn't hear any of it. Not that she'd taken the time to find me another school so that I wouldn't have to give up dance. Not the truth that Cindy had, indeed, probably taught me all that she could. Not the fact that my closeness with Cindy was conjuring Mommy's deepest fear, that she was losing her children the way she had lost so many of the people she loved before.

All I knew was that I didn't want to leave Cindy. To me, Cindy and dance were inextricably linked. And in my mind, without her, my career would be over.

MOMMY CALLED CINDY THAT Sunday night to let her know of her decision. I could go to my dance classes at the studio the next day, but then she expected Cindy to drop me off back home. If that was a problem, Mommy, who now had a car, would come and get me herself.

That was it. Good-bye.

That night my head throbbed and spun. Lying on the couch, I thought of the room I shared with Wolfie. On the wall hung one of those caricature sketches that street artists draw, where you pose, they scribble, and then they hand you a portrait that usually looks nothing like you. Cindy had had such a drawing done of Wolfie and me.

I wonder if Cindy will let me take it, I thought, tears filling my eyes.

I didn't bother to put on my pajamas. I lay where I was and fell asleep, knowing that I'd never again return to the room where I'd been lulled to sleep by Wolfie's soft, steady breath.

The next morning, Cindy drove to the motel to pick me up.

In the car, she looked somber. I suddenly felt scared.

"Misty, have you ever heard of emancipation?" Cindy asked.

I knew that the word literally meant freedom. But what was she getting at?

"A lot of child performers become emancipated," she explained. "It's something they seek to have independence from their parents, when they feel they can make better decisions than them about their careers and their lives."

The Copeland clan (*clockwise from top left*):
Doug Jr., Chris, Erica, and me

LEFT: My very first time on pointe, which Cindy was confident (and quick) enough to capture on film. RIGHT: A *pas de deux* class at Cindy's studio. In the background, you can see Jason—this was one of the days he decided to come to class.

Dancing with Ashley Ellis. This was from my first week at Lauridsen, when we were so fascinated by our similarities. We were like sisters—at ABT, they called her "the white Misty."
INSET: The Bradleys and me. Proof that I was never different to them, just a part of the family.

Lola's warm heart. She was so nurturing and natural in her affection from the start.

I was photographed during my ABT audition. In the background, you can see Jared Matthews and Craig Salstein, both of whom are also now soloists!

Soul mates. Leyla and I were inseparable.

Eric—my brother at ABT

My family. *Top row:* Miranda and Tom (the Cantines' daughter-in-law and son); *middle row:* Lindsey, Jeff (Erica's husband), me, Aiden Cantine (the Cantines' grandson), Sofie Cantine (the Cantines' granddaughter), Erica, Mariah, Mom; *bottom row:* Liz, Chris

With my father, Doug, in Chicago

Olu

Legendary ballerina and mentor Raven Wilkinson and me in my apartment, after interviewing her for a documentary

As the Firebird, with Herman Cornejo
INSET: In the ABT costume shop, being fitted for my Firebird headpiece

Back where I started—with a group of talented
young dancers from the Boys and Girls Club

Onstage as an odalisque in *Le Corsaire*.
I've danced this role ever since
I joined the company.

My heart began to pound. A light was dawning, but I wasn't sure I wanted to see what it illuminated.

"You're not going to class," she said gently. "I want you to meet a friend of mine."

We drove to a coffee shop near the dance studio. Sitting at a table, drinking a glass of water, was a man dressed casually in a polo shirt and jeans. He had a stack of papers in front of him. He smiled as we sat down.

His name was Steven Bartell, and Cindy explained that he was an attorney. Steven patiently began to explain to me exactly how emancipation worked.

Because I was under eighteen and we lived in California, I would have to petition the court to be declared an emancipated minor. A judge could grant it immediately, or the petition might require a hearing. If my request was ultimately approved, I would then be able to make decisions about my dance career, about where I lived—about nearly everything, really. It wouldn't be up to Mommy. It wouldn't be up to Cindy. It would all be up to me.

He paused.

"Do you think you want to do this, Misty?" he asked. "Cindy thinks it's in your best interest, but you're the one who has to decide."

All these years later, I still cannot remember what I felt in that moment. Mommy had not always been the mother that I felt that she should be, but she was still mine. I loved her, and I knew that she loved me. I didn't want to hurt her.

But did she really know what was best for me? Often it seemed we children had to take care of her and each other, instead of the other way around.

I had to make a choice.

And in that moment, for the first time, I chose myself. I chose ballet. And that meant staying with Cindy.

"Yes," I said softly. "I want to be emancipated."

The rest is all a fuzzy nightmare.

I know that Steven Bartell quickly gathered the papers that had been sitting on the table in front of him. "We're going to need to contact your mother," he said. "And you shouldn't be around when we do. I'm sure she'll calm down once she gets past the initial shock, but in the meantime, Cindy wants you to stay with some friends."

Cindy hustled me into her car and drove me to the home of another student at the San Pedro Dance Center whom I barely knew. If the girl's mother offered me something to eat, I had no appetite. They tried to make small talk at first, but I was distracted, dazed. I would respond when spoken to, but mostly I just sat, numb, watching the TV.

"What are they going to say to Mommy?" I wondered, my stomach in knots and my head pounding. "What's Mommy going to think? How will my brothers and sisters feel?"

I found out later that Mommy called the police and reported me missing. In her frantic search, she also apparently reached out to the media. I can only imagine what might have been said on the six o'clock news.

"Misty Copeland, a local girl who's been recognized as a ballet prodigy, is missing," the anchor would say.

"The girl's mother has reported her disappearance to the local police. She believes that her daughter's dance instructor, Cynthia Bradley, is involved."

Then they would have shown Mommy, terrified and angry.

"I haven't been able to reach her. She was staying temporarily with her dance teacher, but is now moving back home, and I'm sure Cindy Bradley has something to do with this."

I felt like I was going to throw up.

I stayed with that family for three days, fearful I'd be in trouble for running away. Then, one morning, Steven Bartell showed up.

"Misty," he said, "I need you to get your things."

We met with two police officers, who then drove me to a local police station. Soon after, Mommy arrived. She grabbed me and held on tight.

I walked out of the police station with my mother. I feared I was leaving ballet behind forever. Mommy got behind the wheel, and I climbed in beside her, sobbing hysterically. My world was ending.

❦

LIFE HAD NOT JUST turned full circle. It had sped up, then rotated in reverse.

I was back with my family, back at the Sunset Inn.

The motel walkways were still covered with grime. The room we shared was unkempt, cluttered. At night, blanket or sleeping bag in tow, I struggled to ferret out a spot on the living room floor where I would sleep among my siblings. This was the life that Mommy had forced me back to. A few days before I'd been in a beautiful condo, the soft swish of the surf lulling me to sleep. Now, the bleat of highway traffic woke me from my dreams. I went days without eating an apple or even so much as a canned vegetable. I thought Mommy was selfish and cruel, sacrificing my well-being, my opportunity, to soothe her own battered pride. I overflowed with anger and resentment.

How could she do this to me?

Those first days back home, I would lock myself in the bathroom for hours, sitting on the edge of the bathtub, crying. I didn't want to be around my mother. I didn't want to be around my brothers and sisters. I just wanted to be left alone.

But that was going to be impossible. Even though I was back home, our emancipation drama was in only its first act.

Mommy took the Bradleys to court, hiring the well-known attorney Gloria Allred to represent her. Hiring Gloria Allred was like posting the details of your life in neon on the Sunset Strip. Cameras and reporters were everywhere, hovering near the Torrance courthouse, even gathering outside our front door.

Mommy accused Cindy and Patrick of manipulating me into filing for emancipation and said that she wanted a restraining order to keep the Bradleys away from me for good. Though I didn't want anything to do with it, Mommy forced me to accompany her to court. She and Gloria felt my presence reinforced their position. Bewildered and scared, I would look down at the floor to avoid the camera flashes and prying eyes, but every once in a while I would steal a glance at Cindy and Patrick. They stared straight ahead, but I noticed Cindy's lips trembling. It was hard to see them looking so tired, hurt, and sad.

At first, Cindy and Patrick fought back. They told the press, the court, and anyone else who would listen that they had just wanted me to have the kind of home life and exposure that a young, talented ballerina needed. That kind of stability and refinement, they argued, was something that my mother—single, with six children and little income—could hardly provide. Cindy later told one reporter that if I had wanted it, she would even have adopted me.

But by the fall, the fury had begun to subside. Through Gloria Allred, I formally withdrew my emancipation petition. And Mommy's restraining order request went nowhere because Cindy and Patrick hadn't harassed or threatened my family or me.

"The dismissal of the emancipation petition accomplished the main goal of keeping the family bonds intact and strong, without interference by third parties," Allred said in a statement at the time. "In the sworn declarations filed by the Bradleys in response to the restraining order, they said that we have not and will never do anything to interfere with Misty's relationship with her mother. . . . Since Misty's mother has accomplished all of the goals that she intended to achieve when she filed her papers with the court, we have chosen not to proceed to seek an injunction in this matter."

Except for a few rare occasions, I wouldn't see Cindy or Patrick again for over a decade. Had I known that night would be our last, I wouldn't have spent it sleeping blissfully in my bed. I would have gathered them to me, squeezing them tight, and not letting go.

❧

WHEN MOMMY AND THE Bradleys decided to stand down, it ended the fight in the courts. But the battle in my mind and spirit raged on.

In September, I returned to San Pedro High School, a

sixteen-year-old eleventh grader. Being there was different from before. Now, everyone knew my secrets.

All through my school years, I had tried to appear perfect. Arriving at school long before the first bell rang, being the most earnest hall monitor Dana Middle School had ever seen, demanding the same excellence from my drill-team charges that I demanded of myself.

I didn't allow anyone, not even my best friends, to get close enough to see how spoiled my life was underneath. I didn't invite them to Robert's house, which was scarred by hostility and violence, or to the random apartments or the shabby motel room my family shared. My classmates didn't know about the series of men rotating through my mother's life, or the foraging for change when the food stamps were spent. They had no idea that my cheerleading sister and athletic brothers, so carefree during the day, had to come home at night and act like parents to me, Lindsey, and sometimes Cameron.

Now the curtain had been thrown open for the world to peer in. Misty Copeland, the ballerina girl, had an upside-down life.

Looking back, even I recognize that my story was a sensational one. Like the most tragic ballets, there was a central character, innocent and bright, being pulled and pushed between two worlds. Would I emerge triumphant, like the Firebird? Or would I be more like Giselle, who succumbs to a broken heart? My ending had yet to be written.

Newspaper columnists opined about my future and who was best to steer it. There were articles in the *Los Angeles Times* and segments on the entertainment show *Extra*. On the local television news, sandwiched between the latest shooting and an ordinance being voted on at City Hall, there were shots of the Sunset Inn and images of me spinning in tulle and chiffon, while my world crashed around me.

We even got calls from producers who were interested in doing a TV or feature film about the whole ordeal. Mommy retained a lawyer to sift through the offers.

Meanwhile, I had to get through the first days of school at San Pedro High. My classmates greeted me tentatively.

"Hi, Misty," they murmured nervously.

"Glad you're back," one girl, who had danced with me on the drill team at Dana, said a tad too cheerily.

They were trying to be nice, to act as if it all was no big deal, but for someone as shy as me, so fearful of being judged, it was hard to imagine a worse scenario.

But there was nowhere to hide. I had tried to run and failed. Now, just as in my first competition, I needed a backup plan so my audience wouldn't know how much I was faltering inside.

I remembered Paloma Herrera, dancing her *pas de deux* in *Don Quixote*. At the conclusion of the ballet, she didn't take her partner's hand. Fierce and independent, she stood apart and balanced on her own.

I knew that's what I would have to do now. Recover, hold my head up high, and balance on my own.

IT WAS IMPORTANT TO me that I not miss too many days of dance class. So a couple weeks after going back home to Mommy, I was thrilled to be in a studio again, turning my focus back to ballet.

Named for its founder and director, Diane Lauridsen, the

Lauridsen Ballet Centre wasn't affiliated with a ballet company. It was a small studio, but it had a strong reputation in Torrance, California.

I believe Diane had prepared the other students for my arrival. They didn't turn their noses up at "the prodigy," or gawk at the girl in the middle of a custody tug-of-war. Instead, they embraced me easily, like family. I was relieved to be on familiar ground, immersed in ballet, surrounded by others content to spend hours stretching and straining in pointe shoes.

The first two girls I met there remain two of my closest friends to this day: Kaylen Ratto is my partner in my dancewear business, and Ashley Ellis went on to join ABT a year after me and was a member of the corps for five years. She's now a principal dancer with Boston Ballet.

It is rare to have two students from a school that was not professionally oriented end up performing with a major company. But it happened. And Ashley and I, as well as Kaylen, were inseparable from the beginning. They didn't speak of my ordeal, though I'm sure they knew all about it. Their friendship was like a salve, warm and healing.

I remember that Diane allowed my mother to throw me a sweet-sixteen party at the studio. My new dance mates were invited, and the Cantines. The Lauridsen Centre closed its doors early, and there were dangling decorations and a table filled with potato chips and cake.

But I still suffered migraines whenever I was under stress, and I had just gone through the most difficult period of my life. I lay down in a darkened back room for two hours, embarrassed and upset, while the party went on up front.

I heard later that everyone had a blast.

THOUGH DIANE AND THE students were welcoming, I was hardly treated with kid gloves when it came to my dancing. Lauridsen was a small school, but the technique taught there was at a very different level from what I'd experienced at Cindy's. The painful truth was that, despite my being deemed a prodigy, the fact that I had been dancing only two years and was the best student at the San Pedro Dance Center was a testament to that school's limitations. More so than anything, the level of healthy competition from the dancers around me in San Pedro was hardly that of the more advanced students at Lauridsen.

It was different studying with Diane. Even after being exposed to the rigors of my six-week summer program in San Francisco, Diane's school opened my eyes to the realization that my technique needed polishing. I quickly had to shift gears, to refine, and in some cases even to relearn, various steps. To more quickly push my second foot beneath my first as I leaped in an *assemblé*, to make sure that when I swept my pointed foot around in a circle in my *ronds de jambe*, I etched the letter *D*, instead of drawing a squishy sphere.

I was eager to learn and work hard to catch up, to get as close to perfection as I possibly could. I had no time ever to preen and rest on my laurels. Still, if I'd had an ounce of attitude, Diane would have doused it.

Diane never let anything slide. She reminded me over and over again how much work I still had ahead. "Don't sit into your hyperextended knees," she said as she softly nudged their flexible backs as a reminder.

"Straighten your back," she'd command. "Push through your turn."

Cindy had always treated me like her little superstar, pushing to showcase my talent. Not worrying about the social politics that impacted even her small ballet school, Cindy never allowed anyone to convince her otherwise. If that meant losing a board member donating thousands of dollars because their kid was not being featured, then so be it. But Diane and her studio worked differently. I was just another one of the girls in her classes, needing to learn and to work hard, like everyone else.

At that time in my life, I think I desperately needed to feel that I fit in and was like everybody else. My teacher, my classmates, and my dancing are what kept me sane.

Photographers and reporters would still come to the school occasionally to see me. I didn't like attention that set me apart from my friends. But eventually, they were coming to talk about the various ballet companies that were interested in my being a part of their summer programs—and, I hoped, one day their studio companies—rather than the controversy that had dogged me.

Still, the drama involving my mother, Cindy, and me would have one final, traumatic act before its *coda*.

"CINDY NEEDS TO SHUT her mouth," Mommy said.

It was a constant refrain. Mommy said that Cindy was still talking to reporters and making her out to be a bad, negligent mother.

"We've got to make sure we get our side of the story out there," she said. At times she seemed obsessed in her furor.

One day she told me that she had gotten a call from the producers of *Leeza*, a talk show anchored by onetime entertainment reporter Leeza Gibbons. They wanted Mommy to come on to talk about her initial arrangement with Cindy, how it had deteriorated and led to my eventual disappearance. Mommy agreed, despite my fervent protests.

It turned out that Cindy would also be there, though not in the same room as Mommy, to make sure both got to air her version of events.

I was terrified. It would be the first time I was in the same space as Cindy since those days in court a few months before. I didn't want to relive that experience. It had been so traumatic, and I was just starting to recover. I just wanted to be in the studio, dancing.

I told Mommy I wouldn't do the show. But she reassured me that I wouldn't have to sit on the stage: I could just sit in the audience, and maybe Leeza would walk over and ask me a couple of questions. My brothers and sisters would also be there for support.

I will never forget the day of the taping. Mommy said that she would come by the school to pick me up. So after my last class, I went outside and waited, expecting her to pull up in her cream-colored Honda Civic.

To my horror, a black limousine rumbled down the street, then stopped in front of me. The driver opened the door, and inside I saw Doug, Erica, Chris, Lindsey, and, of course, Mommy. It was exactly the kind of showy display that I hated. I didn't want attention unless I was *pirouetting* on a stage, and now, here in front of working-class San Pedro High, was a stretch limousine.

Everyone—my classmates, even some of the teachers—was now gawking at me, wondering what was happening, where I was going.

I hurried into the car, wishing that it was a shell into which I could burrow and hide. Crying, I began to yell at Mommy.

"A limo? How could you pick me up from school in a limo when you know this is already too much for me?"

The car was silent except for my sobbing.

It all only got worse from there. I sat in the audience, next to Erica, while Mommy took a seat on the stage. Cindy was there, too, but in a back room, visible only on a monitor as a producer interviewed her separately.

Though Mommy had warned me, I was startled when Leeza Gibbons suddenly turned her attention to me, asking a couple of questions. I managed to mutter yes and no before I broke down crying.

That's when Erica, always protective and maternal, stood up and took the microphone.

"You tried to destroy our family," Erica yelled at the monitor showing Cindy's face. "You exploited a little girl, and now you want to act like you're an angel and we're the bad guys. We'll never forgive you for what you tried to do."

It had to have been the longest hour of my life. The limousine later dropped us off at home. And the next day I went to school, trying to keep the spark of anguish that had been reignited from bursting into a full flame.

As I walked down the hallway, several of my classmates approached me. "We saw you on TV," they told me. "Our teacher turned on the show so the class could watch."

I was mortified—I felt naked, exposed. I no longer had

Cindy's home, the San Pedro studio, or school. Nowhere was sacred. But I had no choice but to keep going.

❧

SLOWLY, THE DAYS RESUMED a regular flow instead of their former slow, creeping quality. A few months after I moved back home, Mommy got a new sales job and was able to get a comfortable two-bedroom apartment on a quiet street in San Pedro. That was the first time that I felt we'd ever had a home that was truly our mother's, not available to us based on the whims of some man.

Knowing that, I think we all felt a peace we had never before known. Lindsey and I shared a bedroom, and for the first time in years I could walk to school.

Dance was still the center of my life, but I attended classes only in the afternoons now that I was no longer being homeschooled. Still, I felt the rigor of the instruction and the prowess of some of my fellow students made up for the shorter period of time I was spending in the studio. One of Mommy's gifts to me was a life-size cardboard cutout of Mariah Carey. I pinned it to my wall, right next to a poster of Paloma Herrera.

I began to appreciate Mommy again, how she had made sure to find a new dance home for me with Liz Cantine's help. How she had been able to get back on her feet—buying a car, getting her own apartment. She was finally taking care of our family. I just wondered why it hadn't happened sooner.

There was a photograph on the living room mantel of Gloria Allred holding my hand up in triumph outside the court building in Torrance. By then, the tug of war raged mostly in the recesses of my mind.

And I now had a little perspective, allowing me to unspool the reel of the previous three years.

When Mommy and my brothers and sisters said I had been brainwashed by Cindy and Patrick, I ignored them, or fought them fiercely. Now I was no longer so sure.

I came to believe that while Cindy and Patrick had meant no harm, I *had* been brainwashed, if only a little bit. I grew to believe that I deserved more and that Mommy was not willing or able to provide it. But just maybe, I'd been wrong.

It was a revelation. One day, near the end of that transitional year in my life, I sat down beside Mommy on the couch in our living room. I thanked her for fighting for me, for never giving up on me or on herself. And I apologized for what she must have gone through.

Now that I'm grown, my perspective has changed yet again, to one that is more balanced and completely my own. What I know for sure is that Mommy loved me fiercely, and that the Bradleys had loved me, too. That I wouldn't be where I am without their dedication, their willingness to sacrifice and take me into their family. Without them, I would not have learned to voice my opinion, to feel confident that I had opinions worth listening to. All that, and more, the Bradleys gave to me.

LESS THAN A YEAR after the battle over my emancipation, I would go away to New York for the first time, to participate in ABT's summer intensive program. Jessica would go with me, just as we'd planned the previous year at San Francisco Ballet.

I'd auditioned for the program a few months before. The drill for all the summer intensives' admissions was basically the same. Budding ballerinas would look in the back of *Dance Magazine* to find the schedule of observation classes being held at studios across the country by each major ballet company. The classes were the way potential students auditioned for the companies' summer instruction.

The tryouts usually took place over the course of a single month. Each school required its own particular uniform—*black leotard, pink tights, no distracting colors!* You'd show up at your allotted time, pay a small fee, and be given a big number to wear over your chest. Then you and fifty or sixty other dancers would go through the moves of a typical ballet class, at the barre, in the center, while a school representative stood to the side or behind a table, watching closely.

I was invited to audition for ABT's summer intensive by Rebecca Wright, who was the program's then director. She'd also been one of the judges when I'd won the Spotlight Awards more than a year before. Liz and Dick Cantine took me to the studio, paid the required fee, then waited in the hallway outside with the parents of all the other dancers.

A couple of weeks later I received a letter in the mail telling me that I had been accepted on full scholarship. In June, I headed to New York.

Chapter 7

≋

THE FIRST TIME ANYONE from American Ballet Theatre had seen me, I was fifteen years old and was competing in the L.A. Spotlight Awards.

From the time I sat in front of the television at the Bradleys, transfixed by Mikhail Baryshnikov, Gelsey Kirkland, and the other stars of ABT, I had dreamed that I would one day be a part of that company. I had to walk where Paloma Herrera walked, dance where Paloma Herrera danced.

ABT had been one of the five companies that offered me a scholarship to attend its summer intensive program. But New York had felt too far away at age fifteen, so I headed up the California coast instead. Now, a year later, I was ready to take the Big Apple by storm.

A friend of Mommy's met me at LaGuardia Airport, and we took a cab to where I'd be living, a convent on West Fourteenth Street in New York City's Greenwich Village, with the Carmelite Sisters Teresas of San Joseph.

Some people may have found it stifling, strange, to be a teenager living in a nunnery, the Mariah Carey poster I'd brought with me taking its place on my wall among the rosaries.

But I found it comforting. The structure and order of the nuns' world put me at peace.

The theatrics that had brought such a turbulent end to my San Francisco summer were long over. I felt I could walk anonymously through the canyons of Manhattan, preparing for my next adventure.

The primary dramas in my life now were the ones that I wanted—fitting in with the occasional ballet diva, winning the approval of the ballet mistress, hoisting myself to the next rung on the ladder that would hopefully lead me to a permanent spot within my dream company, ABT.

But one day, I was walking down the street, earbuds in my ears, bopping to a long-forgotten beat, when I caught a man looking at me strangely.

"Hey," he said. "Are you that little girl everyone was fighting over in California?"

New York was a new start for me. No one knew me, I was at ABT, and I could finally start the life I dreamed of. But hearing this man's words made me feel otherwise.

OUTSIDE THE CONVENT'S DOORS was New York City, with its dirty streets and omnipresent cacophony that sounded like an orchestra endlessly tuning its instruments. It crackled with the aggressive energy of people rushing everywhere and nowhere, and the humid air reeked of garbage, urine, and meat frying on food carts. It was my first time visiting a city this big. I had never experienced anything like it.

But behind the convent's pink walls, the nuns were kindly and motherly. They spoke no English, only Spanish, and most of the time I had no idea what they were saying. Each small room had an intercom, and every morning at seven a.m. it would buzz to wake us from our dreams.

BZZZ.

"El desayuno esta listo," a Sister would call. "Breakfast is ready."

We hated that early-morning salute. We wanted to sleep longer. But we loved the breakfasts and dinners that the Sisters prepared for us girls every day.

The dorm, with two narrow beds to a room, didn't just house dancers studying with ABT. There were students from other summer intensives as well. At first I bunked with Margeaux, a girl whom I danced with at the Lauridsen Centre back home. She was attending the Joffrey Ballet's summer program. But halfway through, I began to share a room with my good friend Kaylen, also from my school in California and dancing with the Joffrey that summer.

Then, of course, Ashley Ellis was there, too, dancing alongside me at ABT. It was like musical chairs, with Ashley sometimes staying with Margeaux while I was in Kaylen's room, and then switching back again.

I remember how our legs would ache after dancing all day, and we had to hike up flight after flight of stairs because the convent didn't have an elevator. In the evening, all of us girls would gather—whether training with the Joffrey, New York City Ballet, or ABT—to eat dinner in the basement, where all our meals were served. Then we'd watch movies. Mommy sent videos of 'NSYNC in Concert, and we all drooled over Justin Timberlake.

The first day of the program I was called into the artistic office where John Meehan and Kirk Peterson were waiting for me. Kirk had been a principal dancer with both ABT and San Francisco Ballet and served as the program's resident choreographer and ballet master. John was a former principal dancer with the company and the artistic director for ABT's Studio Company, where junior dancers performed before moving up to the main company.

Kirk spoke first.

"We've heard your story, Misty," he said, "and we want to know more."

I told them about the Boys and Girls Club, how I was hesitant at first but then fell madly in love with ballet. I told them about the thrill of winning the Spotlight Awards, how much I loved playing Clara in *The Nutcracker* and Kitri in *Don Quixote*, how ABT had always been my dream company.

I left out the battle that had gone on between Mommy and Cindy. But they didn't forget. They asked me a little bit about it. I kept it short and sweet, though this was a bit disheartening. People had often known things about me that I didn't share or want them to know. I thought New York wouldn't be this way, but even here I was exposed, vulnerable to being labeled "different."

Still, all that didn't stop them from telling me why they had called me into the office. They told me that I was an extraordinary talent, and John said that he was already planning to invite me to join the Studio Company sometime soon.

I was overwhelmed.

THIS WAS ALSO THE summer that I met Paloma Herrera. I have to say that, at first, I was a bit disappointed.

It must have been lunchtime. We summer students weren't really allowed to wander around ABT's studios, a warren of run-down rooms. The company occupied two floors of a building downtown, at 890 Broadway. There were five studios where we rehearsed. Each of them had two walls covered floor to ceiling with mirrors, and barres were attached to all the walls but one; more barres were stacked like firewood in the back, to be moved when we needed them to the floor's center. A piano was invariably tucked in the corner, and each studio had a television and sound system in the front so we could watch videos to help us with our choreography, as well as old-fashioned wall phones, where we'd line up to order lunch to be delivered from Andy's Deli on our breaks.

The studios that make up the company's rehearsal spaces look like sets taken straight from one of the 1980's dance movies I'd watch with Cindy and Patrick in California. It's one of the few dance buildings that hasn't become super-high-tech and sleek—a total contrast to San Francisco Ballet, for example. It's typical New York, I guess, to have the office building of America's National Ballet Company be as quirky as an East Village apartment building. Like in so many of the aging buildings that crowd New York City, the perimeter of ABT's practice rooms were lined with ancient radiators to keep them warm. They clinked and clanged so loudly in the winter that it was sometimes hard to hear the playing of the piano. And in studio five, one of our two large rehearsal spaces, the windows got so fogged up from the sizzling steam and dancers' body heat that you couldn't see out to Nineteenth Street.

The studios were sweltering in the summer as well. There were air conditioners installed in the windows, but we dancers didn't want them turned on for fear our muscles would get cold and stiff.

There were also two large dressing rooms, one for women and one for men. They were filled with benches and creaky lockers that dancers claimed their first days with the main company and held on to for the duration of their careers there. Our physical therapy room was filled with all you'd find in a high-priced gym, from cardio and weight machines to Pilates reformers. There was also a small massage room, where the company's therapist would rub and knead our tired, sore muscles.

Upstairs, on the third floor, there were two more studios and the company offices housing the artistic staff, stage managers, and company management, as well as the fund-raising, publicity, and education departments, and our executive director.

At lunchtime, I would usually take a walk down the street, pick up soup or a sandwich at a local salad bar, and then come back to the studio, where I'd eat and relax with other dancers before heading back to class.

But one day, for some reason, I felt like exploring. The hallways smelled of sweat and age. I wandered into one of the larger studios, and there was Paloma Herrera, talking on the studio phone.

I expected her to be so much taller, but she was only a few inches ahead of me in height. Her jet-black hair was pulled into a loose bun. And she had one of her legs planted on a chair by a wall, stretching.

Always the ballerina, I thought, awestruck, *even when chatting quickly with a friend.*

She looked just like the diva I expected my idol to be, flexing nonchalantly, pushing her body in a way mere mortals couldn't imagine, as effortlessly as flipping aside her hair.

What do you do when you come face-to-face with your dream? Someone whose picture hangs on your bedroom wall, whose footsteps you've followed, whose performance as Kitri in a ballet you saw long ago inspired you to be here today, three thousand miles from home, in the company where Mikhail Baryshnikov reigned and Gelsey Kirkland danced?

You approach her stealthily, quietly.

"Hello," I finally said, with a voice that fell somewhere between a squeak and a whisper.

No response.

I can't remember if Paloma was still on the phone or had just hung up. What I do recall is feeling a cold vibe from her. I thought that she was just a little bit mean.

They say that it's not a good idea to meet your idols because you find out that they are as human, as moody, as imperfect as you.

But Paloma's aloofness somehow made her even more intriguing, made me even more obsessed. I turned and walked out of the room.

Of course she's a little bit full of herself, I quickly concluded. *She's Paloma Herrera!*

However inauspicious that meeting in a forbidden studio, my momentary encounter with Paloma was just the beginning of our relationship. I feel now that it took a decade to get to know her. But now, having had my own turn in the spotlight, having felt the adulation and also the isolation that comes with being the "only one," I understand why she seemed to have erected a wall around herself.

The spotlight has often been focused on me because I was a late bloomer who turned out to be a prodigy, and perhaps, more than that, because I am a black woman excelling in a white world. Paloma also stood out for being exceptional, a teenage soloist and then principal who went head-to-head with older dancers.

I can only imagine what it was like for her to join ABT at the tender age of fifteen and to have so much expectation heaped upon her shoulders. I can imagine the snubs and slights she must have endured from those other ballerinas as they watched this ingenue move so swiftly up through their ranks.

I can imagine it quite clearly, actually, because I experienced some of what she went through.

Years later, when Kevin McKenzie, the artistic director of ABT, promoted me to soloist at the age of twenty-four, I became the first African American woman to hold that position in twenty years. I made the cover of *Dance Magazine*, the same publication I used to buy and carry in my backpack so that I could read about Paloma Herrera. I spoke to the writer about both Paloma and Gelsey Kirkland: how when I thought of a ballerina, I saw their fluid movements in my head. I told the writer that from the time I discovered ballet at the age of thirteen, Paloma and Gelsey were all that I wanted to be.

After that cover story appeared, it was Paloma's turn to quietly approach me.

"I read the story about you in *Dance*," she murmured, walking up to me one day as I stretched in the studio between rehearsals. "Thank you for saying so many great things about me in the article."

It's funny. In an interview, you talk and talk and talk, somehow not fully realizing that people, including those you are speaking about, will actually read what you said. For a moment I was surprised, even a little embarrassed, that Paloma had read my gushing comments.

But I was also happy that my onetime idol had been flattered that I had appreciated her, that even though I was now a soloist, dancing beside her, I was not too proud to tell the world that I was also a fan and how Paloma Herrera had inspired me.

We smiled at each other, peers. And I can say that we are also very good friends.

WITH ALL THE GIRLS, fun, and friendship, ABT's program was in some ways like summer camp in pointe shoes. But we worked incredibly hard, rehearsing *arabesques* and *pliés* seven hours a day.

Together, Ashley and I would trek the fifteen minutes to ABT's studios on Broadway each morning. Among the 149 young people in the school, she and I were placed in the same levels, and soon after we arrived, we learned the parts we would play in the end-of-summer recital.

Ashley would have a solo. And Kirk Peterson decided that I would perform a *pas de deux* he had choreographed to a Philip

Glass composition, as well as a principal variation in *Paquita*, the story of a gypsy girl who saves the life of a soldier and then discovers that she was born to nobility. It wasn't hard for me to switch styles from Kirk's contemporary choreography to the classical ballet to follow. I know now that ABT has always appreciated my ability to make that transition between diverse styles of dance. Though my primary love has always been for the classic ballet stories I would watch and rewatch with Cindy, my athletic body is just as comfortable with modern movement. This was my first time experiencing anything other than classical ballet, besides my performance in *The Chocolate Nutcracker*, but I loved it.

The other students were supportive and admiring. They believed Ashley and I both had perfect technique, and they called Ashley "the white Misty" because we had similar bodies and dancing technique, having come from the same school.

We were pretty much the stars of the program that summer. The night of the recital, after we'd taken our bows, I was autographing a few pairs of my tattered pointe shoes for some of the other dancers and taking pictures with my friends when I was told that Kevin McKenzie and John Meehan wanted to see me.

I hurried to the stage, where they waited for me.

"You were wonderful tonight, Misty," John said. True to his word, he invited me to join the Studio Company.

I knew John had said that was his intention, but I was still stunned by the offer. I was a junior in high school, just sixteen. But my dream of dancing with ABT was right there for the taking.

I searched to find my voice.

"I have to ask my mother," I said finally.

I practically ran back to the convent so that I could call Mommy. She was uncertain. I needed to finish school, she said, and I had already spent so much time away from the family.

But then she surprised me.

"It's up to you," she said before we hung up. "I think the year will fly by, and hopefully they'll make you the same offer next summer. But it's your dream, and I want you to feel good with the final decision."

I didn't know what to do. I kept stalling, telling Kevin over the next several days that I needed a little more time to figure it all out. He and John said that I would still be able to take classes and earn my high school diploma. And they would essentially offer me a scholarship to cover the costs of my equipment and travel. It was tantalizing, thrilling.

But my big sister, Erica, would soon be giving birth to her first child, a baby girl whom she already planned to name Mariah. And Mommy and I were spending time together, loving each other, enjoying each other, living in a comfortable apartment all our own with my little sister Lindsey, at last. I didn't want to leave them to be all alone in the big city. Not yet.

"I want to finish high school back home," I finally told Kevin and John. "I hope you still want me next year."

They nodded and smiled.

❧

AS A PARTING GIFT, ABT awarded me a Coca-Cola Scholarship, money that would pay for my pointe shoes and training back in Southern California. They later confirmed that I would have a guaranteed spot with the Studio Company when I finished high school.

I returned home excited about my career and eager to finish high school. The months whizzed by. I socialized more with the girls at the Lauridsen Ballet Centre than those at San Pedro High, but when the senior prom appeared on the horizon, Mommy insisted that I go.

Most of my friends at school were Asian, and on Fridays, when they went to meetings of the Mabuhay Club, I would sit at a table on campus alone, except for when Lindsey, now a ninth grader, had time to join me.

I had two potential prom dates, a Korean American friend, and an African American boy who had also asked. I went with my Korean American friend because he had asked me first, still shocked that anyone had asked me at all. I was so shy, the thought of dating left me petrified, and I'd never been out with a boy. I'm not sure I would have even gone to the movies with Justin Timberlake if he'd asked, and I thought he was absolutely adorable.

On prom night, I flat-ironed my hair and put on a long red dress with a slit nearly as long as me. The party was in a ballroom at the Intercontinental Hotel in downtown Los Angeles. I was miserable the whole evening. The nadir came when my date tried to kiss me at the after-party held at one of our classmates' homes. I backed away in disgust. I had never kissed a boy. I had never even held one's hand, unless he was my *pas de deux* partner, lifting and whirling me across a stage.

That June, I graduated, and I couldn't get out of my cap and gown quick enough so that I could pack my bags. I was headed to New York City for good.

This summer intensive program would be a bit different from the one before. By now, I was folded more deeply into the fabric and community of ABT.

Instead of the convent in Greenwich Village, I would stay with Isabel Brown. Little did I know when I took a cab to her brownstone on Manhattan's Upper West Side that her home would also be mine for the next two years.

In the ballet world, Isabel Brown is a legend, part of what is known as the Brown Dynasty. Isabel danced with the company when it was founded decades before She met her husband Kelly Brown, also a dancer, through ABT. Their son Ethan became a soloist and daughter Leslie went on to be a principal with the company. In fact, Leslie coached me through both of my summer intensive programs, and Ethan was still dancing as a soloist when I joined ABT.

I found out during my senior year that Isabel had extended an offer to host me in her home when I returned to New York. It was an extreme honor. She was regal, elegant, and her home was like an abode plucked from the upper-crust environs of *The Philadelphia Story.* There were antiques tucked in the corners and tables made of glistening mahogany.

I would rummage through her bookshelves, fingering ABT programs that dated back to the start of the company. The movie *The Turning Pointe,* starring Mikhail Baryshnikov, Shirley MacLaine, and Anne Bancroft was based on the Brown family, and Leslie had a prominent role.

Cindy had been right. I *was* dining with royalty.

THOUGH WE NO LONGER lived together, Ashley was also back at ABT for the summer, and we again won all of the leading roles for the final performance. For the first time I was able to work with legendary choreographer Twyla Tharp, in whose works I would often dance the lead once I joined ABT's main company.

During the summer intensive program, my time with Twyla was fleeting. What I remember most was her complimenting my fluidity and technique. Twyla coached Ashley and me, along with her protégé Elaine Kudo, for our performance of her seminal work *Push Comes to Shove*, a ballet first staged in 1976 in which Elaine and Baryshnikov starred. I've always had a tie to Twyla. When I was still at Cindy's and would watch old videos of Misha and Gelsey and Natalia Makarova, Elaine Kudo was one of the dancers I adored. I must have been fourteen or fifteen the first time I saw *Push Comes to Shove*, and now I was dancing Elaine's part for Twyla herself! Having her set her wonderful choreography on me was a dream.

It was later, when I became a member of the corps de ballet, that I truly got to know Twyla. With her silver bob and baggy pants and blouses, she had the appearance and physique of an adolescent boy. But unlike some dancers, who deprived themselves to remain tiny and thin, Twyla was always armed with snacks. One of her quirks is nibbling on lunch meat straight out of the plastic Oscar Mayer packaging. She works her dancers into the ground—by the time you get onstage to perform one of her works, you've practiced it so often that there's no element of surprise, just perfect, confident movement. You're almost sick of the choreography by that point, and performances can feel less spontaneous and free because of it.

Still, it's always amazing to watch, and being part of creating pieces with her is an opportunity I never could have imagined I'd have. She is a firecracker with a feral energy and style of movement that I'd never seen before. She especially loved the men in ABT, literally running full speed and jumping on top of them as she choreographed and created. Whenever she showed up to a rehearsal, the boys would strip off their shirts and dance with bare chests glistening, just because they knew that Twyla loved it. She is aggressive, fearless.

In the midst of the summer program, John reiterated how glad he was that I would be joining ABT's junior company. Though my spot had been assured it was still a wonderful relief to hear he continued to believe in me. Then, at the end of the summer, when we finished our final performance and the lights fell, Kevin called me back to the stage, where he still stood. He told me that before joining the Studio Company officially, I would apprentice with the main company and travel with it to China.

I recorded it all in my journal:

Kevin said congratulations on the performance and congratulations on having a contract. I was in shock. . . . He told me that I was special and they would keep an eye on me. He said that he couldn't believe how strong my contemporary work was and how I was so grounded within it, yet so uplifting and strong in classical. It was a great surprise.

Mommy, who hadn't been able to get the time off the previous summer to come to my show, flew out this time to see me in *Push Comes to Shove*. She stayed on to help me prepare for the next act of my life, as a professional ballerina in New York City.

"Do you have a passport?" Kevin asked.

I didn't—no one in my family did—but I would have slept on the sidewalk in front of the passport office to get one, if I had to. I was over the moon. Dancing with the main company at age seventeen, before I'd even completed the Studio Company program, was more than I'd ever dreamed of. Mommy went with me to a local passport office the next day. I was about to turn eighteen, and this would be my first trip out of the country.

WE WERE GONE FOR two weeks, dancing in Shanghai and Taipei, and we also took a side trip to Singapore. As an apprentice, I had a limited contract, performing as a member of the corps de ballet behind the company's soloists and principals. It was an incredible honor to be in that position when I had no professional experience. I performed in *La Bayadère*, as one of the girls in the waltz sequence, and as a flower girl alongside a friend named Leyla. When we weren't rehearsing or performing, Leyla and I went sightseeing, visiting Bihai Jinsha Water Park and Chenghuang Temple.

When I returned home, I officially took my place as a member of ABT's Studio Company. My ascension up the company ladder had begun.

THE STUDIO COMPANY CONSISTED of six girls and six boys who rehearsed, trained, and performed together for a year to prepare to join the main company. We traveled mostly within the States, to a school in Buffalo, to a small theater in Cape Cod. But we also went to Bermuda, shifting our sore feet through the white sand and turquoise surf. The whole experience was like being in paradise. Most of us had danced together in ABT's summer program, and so we had the familiarity and affection of brothers and sisters.

Often, after shows, the dancers would do outreach, speaking to young people who'd been in the audience. To this day, I am teased by many of the dancers who participated in those talks because the students usually directed their questions to me, having seen me on the news during the drama over whether or not I would become an emancipated minor.

"Are you that girl that was on the *Leeza* show?" someone would inevitably ask.

"Yes, but everything's great," I'd respond in a rush, a tight grin plastered across my face. "I went back home to my mom, and there're no hard feelings. Next question?" I was working on putting the past behind me, but I suppose I shouldn't have been surprised that the controversy continued to find its way into my life. Even in Bermuda, I was racked with fear that my lingering stress migraines would get in the way of my Studio Company schedule.

With the Studio Company, I performed the *pas de deux* from *Sleeping Beauty* in almost every show. It was an honor to be Aurora, the lead. I danced it with both David Hallberg, now an ABT principal, and Craig Salstein, currently an ABT soloist.

They loved me in the Studio Company, and I reveled in

its embrace. I was starting to find my individuality. And my voice—hushed through most of my childhood, freed when I was with Cindy, and silenced again as I tried to recover from the trauma of the court battle—was once again emerging.

Now I claimed my identity—I was Misty, the ballerina from ABT! For the first time I was loud, even boisterous. The little girl whose stomach would tremble if she had to give a book report now had an opinion about dance, about music, about everything. I would argue constantly with Renata Pavam, a Studio Company member from Brazil, about who was the better boy band.

" 'NSYNC!" I'd yell.

"Backstreet Boys!" she'd yell back, before we declared a truce and went out to get burritos at Señor Swanky's.

Renata became one of my closest friends and is still with me in the company today as a member of the corps.

But my very best friend in the Studio Company was Leyla Fayyaz. She and I had been the two girls chosen to be apprentices with the main company in China, and we had formed an instant bond. We both loved hip-hop, and we spent much of our free time jamming to Eminem.

Will the Real Slim Shady please stand up?

Leyla and I roomed together in China and throughout our tours with the Studio Company. She was beautiful—of Cuban, Lebanese, and Persian descent—and I thought she had the perfect classical technique and style. We called each other soul mates. We explored New York City together, first as bewildered young girls gawking outside the handful of peep shows that remained in Times Square, and then as young women, going to lounges and dating boys for the first time. We explored the city with all the wide-eyed wonder of visitors from a foreign land. By the time my first full year in New York City came to a close, I had fallen in love with it. Still, Leyla and I leaned on each other desperately. We ventured from the strict structure of ballet, as that was all we knew, to explore the grand world that is Manhattan. Once, we were even stopped by a police patrol in Central Park. They thought we were teenagers ditching high school. We had to explain that we were ballerinas with ABT and show our Metropolitan Opera IDs to back us up. We remained close friends even when she left ABT only after a year to attend Hunter College, and I was there with her as she dipped her toes into the world of study sessions and final exams. I spent many nights with her in her dorm. Not only were we both curious young women, Leyla was also a late bloomer in life, as so many ballerinas are. I couldn't have survived without her. She now works as a segment producer for the FOX 5 *Morning Show* in New York City.

When I was nineteen years old, I was promoted to ABT's corps de ballet.

The corps is an integral part of a dance company. They're the base that helps to weave the tale, coloring the Pasha's dream in *La Bayadère*, filling the forest in *Giselle*. But for most ballerinas, the goal is to soar beyond it, to stand out enough to get a featured part, and hopefully, one day, to become a principal—that small band of stars who are always cast as Kitri, or Sylvia, or Aurora. Advancing from the Studio Company to the corps was like going from the minor leagues to the main team's second string. The chance to be a starter, to be first, was now within reach, if you could just pitch, tackle—dance—your way there.

Within the Studio Company, there had been rigor and a constant quest for perfection, of course, but there had also been a strong sense of camaraderie.

Now I was one of the cattle in the corps. It was intensely competitive. No one in the main company knew that I was a prodigy, nor did they care to find out. Here, my reputation didn't precede me. I had to start from scratch. It was as if each day, in class or rehearsal, I was auditioning, proving myself, for the first time. There was no room for excuses, no coddling because I had come to ballet late. There was no Cindy to root me on, no Lola de Ávila to hold my hand. Many members of the corps were several years older than me (older than those in ABT's present-day corps), and I felt that I had to grow up fast.

I don't think I stood out for the lack of time I'd spent training, but I did have to learn how to pace myself, how to get along with my dancing peers while also fighting for the chance to dance soloist roles. I was intimidated and I felt my voice beginning to shrink inside once again. I felt that the other dancers, and even some of the instructors, were constantly judging me, and that many wondered why I was there at all. Perhaps some of it was in my head, but, despite my camaraderie with Leyla and my love for ABT, I felt very much alone.

Ballet has long been the province of the white and wealthy. Our daily, toe-crushing exercises make pointe shoes as disposable as tissues, and they can cost as much as eighty dollars a pair. I came from a family that didn't always have enough food to eat, and I was nearly fourteen years old when I saw my first ballet. Most of my peers had grown up immersed in the arts, putting on their first tutus not long after they learned to talk. They had summered in Europe while I didn't get my first passport until I was seventeen. Their families had weekend homes. I had spent part of my adolescence living in a shabby motel.

But I also stood out in another, even more profound way. I was a little brown-skinned girl in a sea of whiteness.

Being "the only one" had never bothered me before. Going to temple with Bubby and Papa, peering out from the Bradley's family photographs, vacationing with them in San Diego, I had rarely even thought about how different we looked from one another. But I also realize my blackness didn't stand out to me because it had never stood out, at least in a negative way, to them.

∾

IN SOME WAYS, BALLET companies are like the military, hierarchical and rigid, with long grueling days spent exerting yourself physically.

ABT, like most companies, has a school for students that it hopes to cultivate. Then there is the Studio Company, which is a training academy of sorts for the most promising upcoming dancers. After a stint at that level, most are invited to join the main company, as I was.

The main company consists of the corps de ballet, the roughly fifty members of the company's chorus, and then the top tier of soloists and principals who are ABT's stars. There are no quotas, though the number of soloists tends to hover around a dozen, while there are roughly twenty principals.

ABT has a spring and fall season. In the fall, we perform for three to four weeks in New York, our hometown. While our stage used to be at the City Center, a stone's throw from

Carnegie Hall, we now perform at the Koch Theater at Lincoln Center, near our spring season home at the Met. The spring season spans eight weeks, and sometimes in the winter, we have a *Nutcracker* season, for roughly four weeks, at the Brooklyn Academy of Music.

Though the performance seasons are only a few weeks, we are working all year long. Rehearsals begin in mid-September, and we go on tour, whether around the United States or overseas, as soon as two weeks later. We tour almost constantly, in between our rehearsals in New York City and for two weeks after we complete our spring season in July.

We have about two months off during the summer, but in all, we work thirty-five weeks a year, though those weeks are not consecutive. Eighteen of those weeks are spent rehearsing, and the other seventeen we are performing on the stage.

It is during those off weeks, which we call "layoffs," that I usually do freelance dancing engagements to continue honing my technique and return stronger to ABT for the new season.

Our physical regimen is strenuous. During the weeks the company is working on its repertoire for the season, there's a ninety-minute ballet class every morning to warm the dancers up for the day. Then we rehearse from noon till seven. Most days we get a lunch break from three to four, but not always. For every other classical ballet company at ABT's level, class is mandatory, as much for the company to guarantee that their dancers are staying on top of their training as for the dancers' own convenience. But at ABT it's up to you to take class. Because there are around eighty of us in the company, we would split into two classes for our barre and center work. Though they happen at the same time in studios one and five, you can pick whichever you like better from day to day, whether it's to train with a certain teacher or avoid a classmate's bad mood. We rehearse as a company Tuesday through Saturday, with only Sunday and Monday off.

The schedule is even more intense during the actual performance season. We'll go to the theater to take our morning classes, and then rehearse and perform from ten thirty a.m. to eleven at night. That's the routine, Monday through Saturday.

Even during layoffs, I will still go to ballet class in the morning, and I'll also work out, doing Pilates and perhaps cardio a couple of times a week.

Exercise and ballet class are critical, not only to stay fit, but to demonstrate your prowess and technique so that when it is time to cast the season's ballets, you are kept in mind. As a member of the corps, standing out in class or during the group numbers on the stage is the only way to be singled out for a starring role. We don't audition for parts within ABT. The closest thing to a tryout comes only when a choreographer is creating a new ballet. Then, you and perhaps two dozen others might be selected to help with the work's creation process. As you and the other dancers learn the same movements, the choreographer is able to determine who best fits and executes the evolving part. You want to show you can pick up the movements quickly and are able to adapt to whatever changes the choreographer desires.

But generally, the path to a starring role is less clear and largely beyond your control. Kevin will watch you, silently, in class and onstage, and then decide whether or not to give you a chance. Soloists and principal dancers will usually be told what roles they will be dancing throughout the year, or which they will be learning for future performances, during the mandatory assessment meetings all dancers have twice a year with Kevin and the assistant director. They'll then have a steady, rigorous schedule of rehearsals to learn and perfect their parts.

The process to reach the pinnacle within a company by becoming a principal or soloist is similarly subjective and, I'll admit, a bit mysterious when you're going through it. Though some European companies hold annual auditions for those positions, within ABT, you again are simply observed over time. Then, one day you may be among the fortunate few to get a tap on the shoulder, or an urgent phone call, beckoning you to Kevin's office, where you hear the news that you've been promoted.

❧

I WAS JUST STARTING my climb toward becoming a soloist or principal, the ink barely dried on my first-year contract, when my honeymoon abruptly came to an end.

By then, other choreographers and companies had begun to notice me, and I went for all that I could during that first year's layoff, flattered by the invitations and hungry for every chance to hone my technique.

Often the rehearsals began late and extended deep into the night. One of those late evenings, I was at the Juilliard building in the Lincoln Center complex working with a choreographer on a piece. I remember that it was a contemporary work, so my body was moving in ways that I wasn't used to.

Suddenly, extreme pain exploded in my lower back.

Foolishly, I danced in pain for a couple of weeks before finally going to the hospital for an MRI.

It turned out that I had a stress fracture in my lower lumbar. It was the type of injury that is usually far more subtle, with the breaking occurring over time. Once you notice it, the injury has been building for a year or more. It was unusual that I'd caught it as soon as it happened.

I had never been hurt before, but I knew I had been unusually fortunate. Injuries are extremely common in the ballet world. Every day there is someone who suffers a stress fracture, a pulled muscle, a neck spasm because we are constantly dancing, dancing, dancing. In a company like ABT, we feel fortunate to have so many talented dancers who can fill in as understudies when somebody has to pull out.

But an injury can be as psychologically painful as it is physically painful. One day you're on the stage and you're the star. The next day you're out with an injury and someone else is on the stage, dancing your part. And you're forgotten.

Though we were in the midst of a layoff when I got injured, ABT was gearing up for the next season, and I suddenly got a call from Kevin McKenzie.

He wanted me to come in and start rehearsing with the company. He wanted me to be the lead character, Clara, in *The Nutcracker.*

It would be like a homecoming. My performances as Clare in *The Chocolate Nutcracker* with Debbie Allen had launched me into the spotlight, had helped to cement my reputation as a prodigy. It was a role in a ballet that I loved. I told Kevin that I would be there.

But with my fractured back, I was in so much pain that I ended up having to pull out and relinquish the role.

My healing and recovery from that fracture would take a

long time. Twenty-three hours a day, for six months, I had to wear a back brace. I did everything but bathe in it. Then, there would be another six months spent rehabilitating.

I had finally graduated from the Studio Company to the corps. I had a contract. And now, for the entire first year, I would not be able to dance.

When I returned to ABT's stage twelve months later, I would be heavier, older. I would never be asked to play Clara again.

Yet I didn't know that at the time. Back then, the professional world of ballet was still so new to me that I was blissfully unaware of all that was at stake. And that may have saved me for a little while from the psychological stress that I now so often feel in my career. I was too naive to worry that I would not get another chance, too intent on healing and too excited about the future to fret about another dancer shifting into my spotlight.

This is just something I'm going through, I said to myself. *When I go back, I'll pick up right where I left off.*

A dancer's body is the instrument with which she makes music, the loom with which she weaves magic. But we take our bodies to places they would naturally never go. We make them fly, dance on tiptoe, whirl like a dervish. We subject ourselves to unbelievable strain. And sometimes we stumble. Or break.

❧

Chapter 8

PICTURE A BALLERINA IN a tutu and toe shoes. What does she look like?

Most would say she is a fragile-limbed pixie, with flaxen hair and ivory skin, spinning in pale pink tulle.

Then there is me, with my full breasts, muscular limbs, and a curve to my hips.

In nearly every way, my body was molded for dance. I have legs and arms that go on forever and are as pliable as rubber bands. My neck is long, my head is small, and I have knees that veer backward as I stand straight. Many young ballerinas look at those odd knees with longing, trying to replicate my line. I was born this way.

I'll bet you didn't know that I could fly. I can bounce into the air, then float there a little while, before lighting, softly, on the stage—achieving the balletic grace known as *ballon*.

My body is strong, able to perform *jetés* and *fouettés*, leaps and spins, for hours and hours across the stage and studio floor.

But ballet isn't just about ability or strength. You must also look the part.

That was no longer the case. It's so important for people to understand that just because it's 2014, racism is still real in the world—and in classical ballet. I was so protected as a young girl, but I was one of the lucky ones. It's one of the things that has saved me and gotten me as far as I've come. My confidence was really born out of a naivete about the prejudices that colored the world of ballet. As an adult, I recognize this as such a blessing, albeit a bittersweet one. And there came a time, standing in a chorus line of ballerinas with boyish figures, when my body stood out as well.

I suppose that for much of my youth, I was lucky. I grew up eating whatever I wanted, filling up on Cheetos, burgers, and whatever canned or junk food I could find. Even when I began to dance, I knew nothing of what was required to nurture a ballerina's body as she grew and matured. Cindy made sure that I expanded my palate. But the pasta that came with the shrimp scampi I loved so much was hardly a diet that would keep me slim. At the Lauridsen Ballet Centre, and San Francisco Ballet, the nurturing and guidance I received was focused on my technique, not my diet.

The reality was that just as I achieved the ability to appear suspended in midair when I performed a *grand jeté*, my body was also locked in time, perpetually prepubescent. At nineteen years old, I weighed less than one hundred pounds. And I had never menstruated.

I had gone home to San Pedro to recuperate, and had more fun than I could ever remember. Mommy was glad to have me home and coddled and looked after me in a way that, frankly, she hadn't since I was a little girl. Liz and Dick were also there to look after me and care for me. And I did things that I hadn't gotten the chance to do in high school, either because I was so focused on ballet or because I was too shy to try.

I got my driver's license. I hung out with my close friend Catalina, whom I met those first days at Cindy's school. We'd go to parties on the beach, where we'd sit around bonfires and talk, joke, and laugh until late in the night. I also took my first cruise, traveling to Mexico and Jamaica with Leyla and her family.

The good times were balanced by the monumental effort I put into getting better. I took class from my old ballet teacher, Diane, as well as Pilates to build back my strength and stamina.

I stayed in touch with ABT, and Kevin and the rest of the staff were extremely supportive. I'd travel back to New York every so often to see my physical therapist. Kevin made it clear that I should take my time and heal fully, and that when I had recovered, they would happily welcome me back.

When my second year in the corps came, I was more than ready to return to the stage. I had a new contract, and I went back to New York, eager to dance again with the company.

But I was not the same ballerina that ABT had known before.

During one of my trips back to New York while I was still recuperating, I went for a routine physical; my doctor said he was worried about the strength of my bones and the fact that I had yet to have a period. Though I was not sexually active, he decided there was a need to accelerate things, and he put me on birth control pills.

It wasn't the most natural way of progressing into puberty. Basically, my body was forced to grow. And grow it did. Within a few weeks, I had my first period and gained ten pounds. Where there had been buds that could barely fill a bra, my breasts became full and voluptuous. They were so foreign to me that they were uncomfortably heavy. I was startled when I looked in the mirror.

Once I returned to New York for good, my body had completely changed. I was menstruating. I was heavier, and I had a very full bust. It was a woman's body, and it felt unfamiliar. I soon realized that ABT, too, was searching for the little girl that I had been.

In the corps, you're constantly switching and sharing costumes with other girls in up to three different casts of the same ballets. There isn't time or money for the company to have costumes tailored to each individual dancer and body.

When I first returned to New York, I was to perform in *Giselle* and *Swan Lake*. But the costumes I was given, handed down from other dancers with their boylike frames, were too tight in the chest. The wardrobe staff would have to let a seam out here, another seam there, to make it fit. I was bewildered and embarrassed. I could feel my confidence start to seep away.

I was constantly searching for appropriate bras that would give me support under the costumes but not make my chest too prominent. I needed the right kind of undergarments that would give me room to move and breathe while I danced.

Finally, the ABT staff called me in to tell me that I needed to lose weight, though those were not the words they used. Telling already thin women to slim down might have caused legal problems. Instead, the more polite word, ubiquitous in ballet, was *lengthening*.

"You need to lengthen, Misty," a staffer said. "Just a little, so that you don't lose your classical line."

I was five feet two and just over a hundred pounds. They suggested a nutritionist, but the company would not pay for it, leaving me boxed in. I was trying to survive on a corps member's salary—six hundred and seventy-nine dollars a week—in New York, the most expensive of cities. And now I had this additional pressure to try to hire a specialist to help me lose weight.

I also needed strength and energy for my grueling days of training. I couldn't go on a strict diet that might leave me weak and depleted.

Like so many things that came late in my life—my introduction to ballet, a more mature body, a license to drive for the first time—I was also starting to feel another emotion most young people experience years earlier, often while they are still in high school.

Rebellion.

Who do they think they're talking to? I would mumble to myself after a long, stressful day. *I have so much talent. Why do I have to be stick thin?*

My backup plan was to outdance everyone, to be so technically perfect and unbelievably lyrical in my movements that all anyone would be able to see was my talent, not my breasts or curves.

In rehearsals, I would push through and focus, push through and focus, returning home each day tired to the bone.

But deep down, I knew that the backup plan wouldn't do this time. My body just wasn't right. It wasn't where it needed to be to perform the classical roles I so loved, or to be in a company as prestigious as ABT. That realization ached. And it was usually at nighttime, when I was home, alone, that I got the most emotional.

MANY ASSUME THAT EATING disorders are rampant in the ballet world.

In a profession that is so focused on appearance, where athleticism and a certain aesthetic are key, dancers will, of course, think about their weight. Yes, sometimes their eating patterns will become unhealthy. For young people who join a high-pressure, high-status company like ABT, it can be easy to feel adrift, to feel as if you don't belong. And in your search for stability, it might be tempting to change one of the few things you can control—your body.

But contrary to myth, there are no weigh-ins by company staff. There are no stern warnings to lose weight "or else." I can honestly say that in my thirteen years with ABT, I have known only a handful of dancers who suffered from an eating disorder like anorexia. We could all see it, though we didn't often discuss it. Other than that, my exposure to those illnesses goes no further than seeing a painful story recounted in a Lifetime movie, or reading the memoir of prima ballerina Gelsey Kirkland, who acknowledges struggling with anorexia as well as drug abuse.

As usual, I turned to Leyla for support and as a sounding board. After that first "fat meeting," I was deeply hurt and lost. I cried and cried as she reassured me that, no matter how I felt, I was decidedly not fat. Still, as a young woman, her next instinct was to cheer me up by convincing me to go out clubbing. I needed nothing more than to dance my worries away.

We went to a trendy new club called Bed, where we lounged and mingled on luxurious mattresses. People came and went, introducing themselves to us, sparking casual conversation. A young man sat between Leyla and me and asked each of us what we did. My answer came out as effortlessly as it always had. "I'm a ballerina."

He looked at me strangely. "No way," he said. "There's no way you could be a ballerina and be as big as you are. Ballerinas are thin."

That was the start of my ultimate low.

I feel lucky that it never crossed my mind to starve myself or purge what I had eaten. But in hindsight, I briefly suffered from a disorder of a different kind. I began to engage in emotional overeating.

Thinking I was fat became a paralyzing mental loop, and I was paranoid that everyone could see it. My mental picture of myself became distorted, as if I was looking in a fun house mirror.

I craved large amounts of fattening foods, like cake and hot dogs, but I was too embarrassed to go to a restaurant and order a big meal.

I'm huge, I would think to myself. *What's it going to look like for me to go up to the counter and order two hamburgers and fries?*

So once again, I came up with a backup plan.

The doughnut company Krispy Kreme had a location on the Upper West Side, not far from where I lived, and they delivered, but only in bulk. So I would call and order two dozen doughnuts, the type of order a company would place.

I would then proceed to eat nearly all the sticky pastries in one sitting.

My binges sparked a whole range of emotions. I would feel comforted at first, then defiant as I thought of how I was ignoring the not-so-subtle entreaties for me to lose weight and was choosing to stuff myself instead. *They want me to lose weight,* I'd think out loud, taking a sugar-crusted bite. *I'll eat what I want!*

But in the morning, I'd feel awful, my stomach tight, my body racked with guilt. I would go the studio and have to face my swollen reflection in the studio's mirrors. I stared at myself, hating what I saw. I'd remember what I'd done the night before and feel ashamed.

Then I'd go home and repeat the pattern all over again.

Because I was continuing to dance and work out, I didn't gain weight, but I didn't really lose any, either. Every few months, the staff would once again gently prod me.

"We believe in you, Misty," they'd say. "We want to push your talent, but your line is not as lean and classical as it was before. We'd like to see you get that back."

I began to notice that I very easily built muscle, and so I had to be careful not to bulk up. I learned that I could do cardio exercises but could not use any resistance when I did.

Gradually, I began to find my balance. It was far from instantaneous. In fact, I think it took me roughly five years, truly, to understand my body, what worked and what didn't. I continued to do Pilates to build strength in my core. And I learned that my diet was probably 60 to 70 percent of what was causing me to gain more weight than I wanted. I came to understand that it played a bigger role than either my workouts or my dancing. So I set about changing my eating habits.

I try to stay away from salt, white sugar, and flour. I don't eat empty calories, like potato chips or my once-beloved doughnuts. I can't limit my mealtimes to certain hours since my schedule can be so busy and erratic, but if I'm focusing on a particular role, I won't drink alcohol. And about four years ago I stopped eating beef, pork, and chicken. When I made the switch to strictly seafood, I saw a huge difference physically.

I've learned to take care of my body, my instrument, to accept it while ensuring that it's in the best shape for me to give my all in every performance.

As a dancer, performing is my life. When I can't dance, I feel lost. So I've had to find that balance that allows me to excel but not push beyond what my body can handle. I know that, as tempting as it may be to keep going and going, putting too much pressure on my instrument could end my ability to dance at all.

There is also a painful memory that bolsters me, reminding me that I am much more than my body.

When I was sixteen or seventeen, I got into an argument with my clever, older brother Chris, who would one day be an attorney.

"What do you know anyway?" he screamed at me. "Dancers are dumb. All they do is use their bodies, not their brains."

His words stung. I remember feeling so hurt, I could barely respond. I knew that he wasn't the only person who felt that way, that he was one of so many others who would never understand all that it took to be a dancer. How we had to meld so many parts—our brains, our emotions, our bodies—to put on a performance that hid all the strings, leaving only stardust for the audience to see.

Chris's words have stuck with me to this day. I feel as if I'm always trying to prove, whether I'm performing onstage or doing interviews with people who don't know much about dance, how intense, multidimensional, and unique this art form is. How much thought it takes, and how much love.

I had breasts, and muscles, but yes, I was still a ballerina. I noticed other dancers who also had more womanly busts, more muscular physiques. And ABT, seeing how hard I had worked, how well I was performing, eventually stopped asking me to lengthen. They came to see things my way, that my curves are part of who I am as a dancer, not something I need to lose to become one.

Chapter 9

❧

THERE ARE TIMES WHEN it's important to seize the spot-light on the ballet stage. Having a musicality in the way you move, allowing the audience to see only the magic and not all the nuts and bolts, is what makes you a star.

But at other times it's important that you blend in. Ballet companies will base a significant part of their decision about whether they want you on the length of your legs, the swoop of your neck, and how those proportions echo those of your fellow dancers. Even I have to admit that there have been times when I sat in the audience and, seeing a dancer with a par-ticularly tiny head, thought to myself that, from the seats down below, she looked odd and out of sync.

In the famous *danse des petits cygnes,* or dance of the little swans, in Tchaikovsky's *Swan Lake,* four dancers—or "birds"— form a human chain, their arms intertwined as each dancer clasps the next dancer's hand in hers. They then proceed, in unison, to perform sixteen *pas de chat,* "step of the cat," leaping sideways while soaring above the stage, legs bent, knees wide apart, and their feet lifted as high as they can go.

It is an acrobatic feat, each dancer displaying grace and dexterity while at the same time she is linked with three others, looking like reflections in a mirror rather than four separate, fallible human beings.

If the contrasts between the dancers are too pronounced, if your torso is much longer than the other cygnets, if you tower above them, some of the synchronicity is lost. The dance appears less perfect, and a bit of the performance's magic slips away.

I understood all that. Luckily, I wasn't significantly taller or shorter than the other members of the corps, and my proportions were deemed ideal for ballet, not only by George Balanchine (who had never met me, after all), but also by Kevin McKenzie, ABT's director.

But there were some who believed there was no place in ballet for a brown swan.

The whispers and talk happened slowly. One Saturday at our studios at 890, on a five-minute break from rehearsal, an older man approached me. It was a day that ABT friends and donors could visit the studios to watch us rehearse. "You do realize you are the only black woman in the company, right?" he said bluntly. "And you very well could be the first to move beyond the corps in many decades." It wasn't unkindly meant, but it was certainly unexpected. I was never approached by anyone at ABT about my color. I was a little taken aback.

A couple weeks later, we moved to the Metropolitan Opera House for the spring season. We had just started rehearsals for a production of *Swan Lake* that would be filmed for an upcoming TV broadcast. I'd been working feverishly on my *pas de chat*, determined to be seamlessly in step with the other cygnets by opening night. I was in the cafeteria on my lunch break when a girlfriend of mine walked toward me. She looked uneasy.

"Misty, I just overheard some of the staff members talking," she said. "Your name came up in reference to *Swan Lake*."

I was confused. "What do you mean? What did they say?"

My friend said that someone commented that I didn't fit in with my brown skin, *especially* in a ballet like *Swan Lake*.

My heart dropped. I didn't understand. I grew worried, especially with the filming of *Swan Lake* fast approaching.

When casting was finally announced, I was not picked to dance in the second act. The "white act."

In the world of dance, there is a genre called "white ballets." *Swan Lake* is one, as is *La Bayadère* and *Giselle*. Their second acts are populated by otherwordly characters—animals or perhaps spirits of the dead—who usually wear white, and it is considered imperative that the corps, and often even the principals, look the same.

It was strange to me to be judged by my skin color rather than my talent or effort. I had seen bigotry in its most vile form living with Robert, hearing the slurs he hurled at my little sister, Lindsey, knowing the ugly things his family said about mine. But that had felt like a surreal, terrible aberration.

My hometown of San Pedro had been a destination for Russian, Japanese, and Mexican immigrants, and my friends and neighbors had come from a multihued pool. I spent years wrapped in the cocoon of a Jewish family, and Cindy always made me feel that I was even more beautiful because of my sun-kissed skin and bushy curls.

Now, suddenly, my blackness was a problem.

Raven Wilkinson, a mentor of mine whom I revere, became the first black American to be a full-time member of a large ballet company when she joined the Ballet Russe de Monte Carlo in the 1950s. Often when she performed, she would literally have to paint her face white. Half a century later, I have often had to do something similar.

At first, I took it in stride as part of the performance, and I didn't mind much. To appear ethereal and ghostlike in the white ballets, all of the dancers dusted their faces with white powder. But for many performances, playing a goat in *Sylvia*, or a sylph in *Giselle*, I was painting my skin a completely different color, taking the ivory base foundation used by one of the other girls and layering it on my face and arms to lighten my skin.

It became a joke among the other dancers.

"You're the only black girl, Misty, but you're always playing an animal that has to be white," one of my corps mates would say with a giggle.

I would usually laugh along. Until after one too many performances, one too many makeup applications, I began to think that it wasn't so funny.

❧

IN 2007, THE YEAR that I would be promoted to soloist, an article appeared in the Sunday edition of the *New York Times*. The headline was "Where Are All the Black Swans?"

It spoke of black ballerinas' thin ranks in American companies. Of how Tai Jimenez became the first member of Dance Theatre of Harlem to find a home with a mainstream classical ballet company, Boston Ballet. And of how

ABT and the New York City Ballet had told her they didn't want her.

The article also told Raven Wilkinson's story of meeting discrimination with defiance and grace. There was a photograph of the gorgeous ballerina Aesha Ash, who had danced in New York City Ballet's corps but moved on after being told that she had gone as far as she ever would. And there was Alicia Graf Mack, who was also turned away by ABT and New York City Ballet before joining Alvin Ailey American Dance Theater.

By then, I had been in ABT's corps for six years. That article was the first thing I'd ever read that reflected the heartbreak and loneliness I felt inside. I'd never before read such a perfect articulation of what I was experiencing: that there were many people who seemed not to want to see black ballerinas, who thought that our very presence made ballet less authentic, less romantic, less true.

The story made me sad and angry. But it was also, somehow, affirming. I was not alone after all. Others had come before me, sometimes in far worse circumstances. Raven Wilkinson had to contend with the Ku Klux Klan as she attempted to dance in the South, eventually having to leave the company because of threats. Unable to find work in this country, she would move to Holland and dance with the Dutch National Ballet.

Her story—all of their stories—made me want to fight even harder to become a soloist, to become a principal, to attain my dream.

I WAS OFF ON Monday, the day after the article appeared, but I was back in the studio Tuesday morning.

Walking to my first rehearsal, a young woman in the company who was a friend of mine rushed toward me.

"Did you see that stupid article in the *Times*, 'Where Are All the Black Swans?'" she asked me in a tone that was more accusatory than curious. "What are they talking about? What a dumb story."

I couldn't speak. I felt dismissed, and even more alone. Was she truly so clueless? If she, a friend, didn't understand my struggles, who else would? The fact that she, like most of the company, liked me and yet could still say what she did so nonchalantly starkly showed how blind most ballet dancers are when it comes to matters of race.

I turned away quickly, my eyes welling up with tears. I felt my way down the hallway and found an empty studio. Closing the door, I began to cry like my heart was breaking. Because it was.

No one understood. Along with all the other insanely hard things that came with being a dancer, the pressure to look perfect despite being in crippling pain, the need to push your body to the brink of injury in the pursuit of excellence, the tsk-tsking of dance masters and critics and patrons, I also had to deal with the snubs, smirks, and insensitivity of people like that girl, with whom I shared a stage but who didn't know a thing about the road I'd traveled. No one got it. No one cared.

There were no other black women at ABT for me to connect with. And my dear friend Leyla soon left the corps. So I often hung around the black boys who came through the company, one or two at a time, lighting for a short while before inevitably moving on.

Danny, Jerry, Dante, Jamar. They all came and went while I stayed.

And then there was Eric Underwood. He was the one with whom I forged the strongest bond.

Eric had grown up in Washington, D.C. in a lower-income but loving family, like mine. Also like me, he had been led to ballet by what only could be serendipity. Or was it destiny?

He was already fourteen years old when he went on an acting audition for a spot in a local arts school. He was trying to avoid going to his neighborhood school, which was violent and lacking academically. The acting tryout didn't go so well, but when Eric walked out, he saw some girls getting ready for their dance audition, and he suddenly thought that was something he could do.

He made it, and that was it. Eventually, Eric would perform with Dance Theatre of Harlem and ABT, and he is now a soloist with the Royal Ballet in London.

We clung to each other. We'd grown up listening to the same music: New Edition, Toni Braxton, Mariah Carey. We had our own secret code, whispering to each other in the lingo we spoke with our siblings back home. We were like brother and sister, bonding over our shared affection for R & B and hip-hop. And we had our own " 'hood" thing, on Friday nights, going to Red Lobster or BBQs, where we'd feast on shrimp, burgers, and ribs to our hearts' content.

There was no translation needed with Eric, no need to explain. If we heard something that seemed a bit callous, a bit racist, we would exchange glances, and there was comfort in knowing someone else had heard the bad note, the off key. We were the only ones who understood the weird moments that arose because we were African Americans in a lily-white world.

One day, Eric had a meeting with Kevin McKenzie about his hair.

When Eric returned from Kevin's office, he tapped me on the shoulder, and we quickly walked together outside.

"He wants me to grow my hair long."

We both roared with laughter, giggling until our eyes watered and our stomachs hurt.

Eric had tried his best to explain to Kevin that if he grew his hair, it wouldn't grow long. Rather it would grow "out." We laughed because we knew if he'd done it, he would have had a huge afro. Was it more fitting to have a short hair cut in the eighteenth-century setting of the ballet, or to look like a member of the Jackson 5 dancing on *Soul Train* in the 1970s?

We were able to make fun of it all, though the harsher reality was that we were constantly misunderstood. It could be exhausting. As black people, we are supposed to tiptoe around situations, to shrug off insults that are at times naive, at times intentional. It's like another dance to perform, making sure that the white people around us never feel guilty or uncomfortable.

Surrounded by dancers who were sometimes my friends and often my competition, I felt more alone than I ever had. But gradually, a group of women began to emerge in my life who became sounding boards and pillars I could lean on when it all felt like too much.

The woman I considered my first real mentor after I'd joined the corps was Victoria Rowell, a former ballet dancer turned actress who continues to be involved with ABT.

Rowell had endured her own challenges as a child, having spent time in foster care. She grew up to dance with ABT's Studio Company before moving on to modeling and acting. She has appeared in numerous television shows and films, but she's perhaps most recognized for her role as Drusilla Barber on the soap opera *The Young and the Restless.*

ABT had traveled to Hollywood for a handful of performances. One night, after I came off stage feeling stressed and exhausted, I found a note with my name stuck to the pin board.

"Please call me," it read. It was signed Victoria Rowell. Below her name was her phone number. I knew of her, of course, and was awestruck that she had reached out to me.

Being in Hollywood, I was only an hour or so from Mommy's apartment . . . but still a world away from my family. Though I know they would have tried, I believed it was impossible for my mother and siblings truly to understand the unique pressure I was under. My late-budding body had suddenly bloomed, and I was still in the midst of my struggle with my weight. I was pushing through grueling practices, all the while trying to quell the self-doubt crowding my thoughts. I was also a bit embarrassed. This is what I had wanted: to dance with ABT, to be a professional ballerina, to live in New York City. I'd almost run away from home to pursue it. Now that I had it within my grasp, how could I complain? And Mommy was so proud, more effusive than she had perhaps ever been. I didn't want to let her down.

So I welcomed Victoria's invitation. When I called, she asked me to come to visit, and she sent a car to take me to her beautiful house in the Hollywood Hills. I believe her children were already sleeping, but Victoria and I sat up talking nearly all night.

I saw a beautiful, successful black woman, a ballet dancer who was now not only making her way but thriving in the cut-throat world of Hollywood. I remember thinking, *There is actually someone out there whom I can relate to.* She was the first person to take the grown-up Misty, with her grown-up experiences, her grown-up challenges, under her wing. We have had many conversations over the years, often on the phone, sometimes over a hearty lunch or dinner. She remains an angel in my life to this day.

Another mentor of mine is an African American woman who was a member of ABT's board of trustees.

Susan Fales-Hill, a descendant of a *Mayflower* passenger, is akin to black royalty. The biracial daughter of Broadway chanteuse Josephine Premice and Timothy Fales, the scion of a New England family whose roots date back to Plymouth Rock, Fales-Hill is a prominent socialite with all the poise, polish, and pedigree that goes with it. She's the type of woman who's a must-invite to every charity gala, and she resided with her banker husband and daughter on the swanky Upper East Side. Yet Susan emanated a light that wasn't inherited, but was entirely her own. She is a graduate of Harvard, a published author, and worked as a writer on *The Cosby Show.*

She is also perceptive. Susan could see that I was faltering, questioning my purpose in ABT. One day she took me aside for a chat.

"You know, many of the board members talk about you," she said with a warm smile. "They feel you are one of the most promising dancers in the company. That you have a future that is unbelievably bright. I agree."

Susan would eventually become my sponsor, one of those behind-the-scenes patrons who make sure dancers have all that they need, from emotional support and guidance to simply someone to chat with at company events. It is a wonderful, ongoing gift. But what I cherish most were her words of reassurance, her ability to recognize and feel my pain, and her desire to share with me kind words, from not just her but from others on the board, to lift me up. She made me feel as if I had a vital role to play within ABT. She gave me the strength I needed to keep pushing, to keep waiting for my turn in the spotlight.

∞

DESPITE MY KINSHIP WITH Eric and the other black dancers to occasionally pass through ABT, and wonderful mentors like Susan Fales-Hill and Victoria Rowell, I continued to feel frustrated and mostly alone. I was putting in eight-hour days, straining my body beyond the point of exhaustion, but the harder I pushed the more I felt I was standing still.

The bitter truth is I felt that I wasn't being fully accepted because I was black, that Kevin and other leaders of the company just didn't see me starring in more classical roles, despite my elegant line and flow.

My Balanchine body was no more, I was crumbling under the pressure from the staff, and I felt there was no one I could approach to guide me. None of my teachers or mentors back home—not Cindy, not Diane, not Elizabeth—had ever danced in a company on the level of ABT. I was no longer a big fish in a small pond, and I was sinking.

I began to contemplate leaving.

I briefly considered moving over to the New York City Ballet, the company that George Balanchine had founded. I was casually acquainted with one of its dancers who offered to talk to the company's director, Peter Martins, and encourage him to come see me perform. I told him that would be great.

That I even entertained the thought showed how desperate and unwanted I felt at ABT. The New York City Ballet was the only company that rejected me for its summer intensive program back when I won an L.A. Spotlight Award at the age of fifteen. It was also the company where the great Aesha Ash languished, eventually leaving and joining a company in San Francisco after never rising above the corps.

Clearly, I was grasping at straws.

Then there was another option that emerged in the summer of 2004 that was far more appealing and that, for a moment, I seriously entertained.

Arthur Mitchell was the legendary cofounder of Dance Theatre of Harlem, the first African American classical ballet company.

He had been New York City Ballet's first black dancer and was its only African American performer for fifteen years. During that time, he became a principal, dancing in *A Midsummer Night's Dream*, *The Nutcracker*, and *Agon*, a ballet where the *pas de deux* was choreographed specifically for him and the ballerina Diana Adams by George Balanchine himself.

But after Martin Luther King Jr. was assassinated in 1968, Mitchell went home to Harlem, wanting to introduce the art form he loved to the children there. A year later he launched Dance Theatre of Harlem in a church basement.

Dance Theatre of Harlem had offered me a scholarship to

attend its summer program the year I won my Spotlight Award, and a few years later, when I had moved to New York and was dancing with ABT, my friend Eric Underwood told me that Arthur wanted to meet me.

The two of us went to Dance Theatre of Harlem's Manhattan studio to take a class with the company.

One of the many great things about ballet is that the structure of a basic class is consistent throughout the world, be it barre, center, the slow movements that are *adagio*, or the whip-sharp motions that are *allegro*. At Dance Theatre of Harlem, Eric and I danced the complicated combinations that you'd find in any class for professional dancers. And afterward, I took another class, in *pas de deux*.

Arthur, soft-spoken and regal, observed me. I later jotted down his words of praise in my journal.

"He had a lot of good things to say about my dancing and his company," I giddily scrawled. "He reminded me of how special it is to be an African American ballerina. [He] said don't let them take you over. Walk into the room knowing you are the best. Shoulders back, chin up. Their attitudes will totally change."

That is something I will always remember: "Walk into a room, knowing you are somebody, somebody special. Don't ever let them smash that or pull you down."

A couple weeks later, I once again made my way to Dance Theatre of Harlem's studios and took another class. There were the same demanding expectations, the same intensity emanating from men and women at the top of their art. But there was also a comfort knowing that if you stood out, it was for how you danced, not for how you looked. Afterward, Arthur wanted to speak with me.

He offered me a soloist contract. He wanted me to be his Giselle.

Arthur also told me of the first time he'd seen me dance.

"He said he was in the hospital a couple years ago when he saw this girl on TV," I wrote in my journal. "'She was sitting there with so much confidence, so much spark,' he said. 'That was a ballerina.'"

But, he said, looking at me now, he knew that ABT had sapped my spirit, had doused that spark that had once entranced him.

"ABT had taken that from me," I wrote in my diary. "I need that back. I need to always have that confidence inside the theater."

I knew Arthur was right. I had always been a performer who came alive onstage. Now, I was technically proficient but lacking the fire that had taken me from the Boys and Girls Club to the Metropolitan Opera House in four years.

He told me that I could get it back, that such a spirit was something that burned within black people. "You have it," he said. "You can't be taught it."

I thought that Dance Theatre of Harlem might be the answer, that it would be so much easier to be in a company where I stood out because of my gifts and not the color of my skin. At last, I'd be the lead in the classical ballets that I loved: *Giselle, Sylvia, Cinderella*.

I wanted to run away from ABT and into Arthur Mitchell's arms. Why not? I admired him immensely and cherished his comforting words. Dance Theatre of Harlem was a legendary company, bursting with talent. And I wouldn't have to fight anymore. I would be able to dance the classical parts that I

Life in Motion

loved, Kitri, Clara, Aurora. It was so sweet to hear positive feedback and not the criticism that I felt floated around me, whether spoken or unsaid.

Then I thought about my mother.

I realized that what I'd seen as her strength when I was growing up—the courage not to let the fear of raising so many children alone bind her to unhappiness—was a failing instead; that my mother was always running away, with my brothers, sisters, and me grabbing hold of her shirttails. Now, I was about to mimic her pattern. And that terrified me.

Rarely had running ever solved any of our many problems. There may have been a temporary respite, a momentary sigh of relief. But then we'd look up and find ourselves in a situation that was arguably even worse, leaving us with too much time to ponder what we had done, why we had done it, and how would we ever recover.

I called Arthur a few days later. I told him I was so thankful but I couldn't accept his invitation.

Later that year, Dance Theatre of Harlem closed because of financial problems. The main company would not perform again for nearly a decade.

✀

IN ANOTHER JOURNAL ENTRY where I recounted Mr. Mitchell's offer, I ended my musings with a determination.

"I need to go in there and show them how much better I am," I wrote, referring to Kevin McKenzie and the rest of the artistic staff.

In contemplating Arthur's invitation, I had felt the full

186

MISTY COPELAND

emotional force of how badly I wanted to succeed at ABT. How I couldn't give up, couldn't run away, and if I had to work ten times harder than everyone else, then I would so I'd always know that I'd tried. I'd fought way too hard to abandon my dream of being a principal dancer with ABT. I wanted always to know that I'd stood my ground, whether or not I got my reward.

But I had to keep tamping down the tendrils of doubt, the voice in my head, that would creep up in the dark.

Mommy had always been afraid that I'd given up my childhood for a dream. Sometimes I wondered if she was right.

❧

Chapter 10

WHEN I WAS STRUGGLING, feeling unattractive and over-weight, isolated and alone, I had a refuge right at my doorstep that helped to keep me afloat.

It was New York City.

Of course, I had an intimate circle of dynamic, success-ful black women mentors and friends, like Victoria Rowell, Susan Fales-Hill, and Raven Wilkinson, who helped me to embrace my more womanly, physical self, and to remind me how wonderful my ethnic heritage was even if some couldn't see it.

But when I went out on the streets of New York, I was instantly, anonymously, lifted up, surrounded by a multitude of people who looked like me, from their copper complexions to their bodacious bodies.

Out there, beyond a ballet scrim, people appreciated my curves and could care less whether or not I'd lost weight.

When I moved to New York, I had to fall in step with two

distinct rhythms, the one behind the walls of ABT, and the other outside, on the streets of the city.

It took more than a New York minute for me to learn the razor-edged etiquette of Manhattan, how the subway doors would barely close behind you before you had to find a spot to fix your gaze—an ad for foot cream? the map of the city's tunnels?—to avoid looking a strap-hanging stranger in the eye. Maybe I wouldn't have instantly become a mark, but my naive straight-on gaze would have labeled me a tourist as surely as if I'd worn a sign declaring KICK ME—I'M FROM CALIFORNIA.

I remember riding the train that first summer I was in ABT's summer intensive program. It was packed and unbelievably hot. Body odor, incense, and perfume made for a dizzying blend. And I felt anxious, sandwiched between strangers, sometimes feeling hands on me where they shouldn't be.

That first summer, I would stand on the corner, helplessly looking for the button that would magically change the pedestrian sign from red to green. As I stood waiting for the light to change, waves of jaywalkers would pass me by, darting through speeding cars, knowing better than to wait for permission to cross.

But New York City, all its grit and frantic rhythms not withstanding, became my salvation. Those first months in ABT's corps, when I felt so unhappy, self-conscious, and alone, the city was the one thing that I could rely on. I appreciated that even as it pulsated with electricity, it was always familiar, always the same.

When I stepped out of ABT's studios at 890 Broadway, I felt as if I was just another person. It was nice for once not to stand out, to blend in. And as much as I cared for and appreciated my colleagues, it was great to be able to walk outside the studio and surround myself with people who weren't ballet dancers, who'd had diverse experiences and led lives that weren't defined by private lessons and hovering parents, and who'd found richness and depth in other ways.

Being a ballerina had begun to consume my entire identity, and that made me worry about what I would be—who I would be—if I didn't succeed.

On the most crowded streets of New York, I could put on my headphones and feel independent, empowered—free.

But I also had to make a million adjustments.

I was used to the arid climate of Southern California, warm and dry during the day, cool and even breezy at night. My first summers in New York the heat and humidity wrapped around me like a blanket, sapping my energy.

It was hard to drop my slower California pace, my seaside attire, and pick up the New York rhythm. In California, I always wore flip-flops when it was warm. But my sandaled feet were no match for the endless, reeking puddles that seemed to pop up on every New York street. I performed *petit allegro* all over the city, hopping over those fetid pools, then going home to clean the dirt and grime off the soles of my feet.

THE PLACES I LIVED were also in stark contrast to the apartments, motel rooms, and condos I'd called home in California. After moving out of Isabel Brown's brownstone, I stayed on the Upper West Side, but from then on I lived on my own.

My friends and I called my first solo apartment "the

dungeon." One of the many odd characteristics of life in New York, an insanely expensive city, is that you basically have to pay more in rent if you want an apartment with windows and natural light, things I'd once seen as basic necessities, no matter how shabby my accommodations had been before then. I didn't make much money, and so I was one of the many in the city whose apartment never saw a ray of sunshine.

There were two windows covered in bars that faced a brick wall about five inches away. I had a loft bed that hung above my dining room table, which was actually a child's arts and crafts table I'd bought at Ikea. If you sat up in the loft, you'd bang your head on the ceiling. And the narrow space that passed for a kitchen had the type of tiny refrigerator that belonged in a dorm room. But I loved it all because it was mine.

As were the roaches in my apartment, which were unbelievably huge. Growing up, we'd had roaches in some of the rougher neighborhoods we'd lived in, and they'd always freaked me out. The fact that you could live in such a well-off and desirable neighborhood and have rats and bugs inside was frightening to me and unfamiliar. Still, I wasn't home much. There was too much life to see—to live—outside. I walked probably more than I ever had in my life. And being outside at all times of the day and night, I would often have to make my way through a blast of catcalls.

"How ya doin', sis?"

"Hey! Can I get those digits?"

At first, they were unnerving. I was living alone in the city, and it made me feel vulnerable having strange men leering at me.

But after a while, I began to realize they were mostly harmless and good-natured. You might draw some attitude if you acted snooty. But if you smiled, or said hello, the calls would usually go no further than flirting, ending with "Have a good day."

Some of the attention actually made me feel good after a while. I wasn't fat on the streets of New York. I was desirable and attractive. In fact, my look—dark hair, brown skin, curvy physique—melded seamlessly into the urban rainbow.

It seemed that everyone claimed me as one of their own—African Americans, Puerto Ricans, Dominicans, even East Indians. I loved seeing and hearing the range of hues, accents, and backgrounds mingling and loving one another on the city's streets. I may have stood out among the frail-looking white dancers whom I danced beside, but out here, they were the ones who didn't quite fit in.

I went to Harlem with Leyla, still my constant partner in crime. We ate yassa chicken, the lemony dish that is a staple of Senegal; bought incense from the vendors; and strolled down streets where Malcolm X walked and Adam Clayton Powell Jr. preached.

I remember we went uptown to see the movie *Paid in Full.* As much as I appreciated the operatic treble of *Swan Lake,* I'd grown up steeped in funk, rock, and soul. And I loved everything hip-hop. I don't even think *Paid in Full* was showing anywhere lower than 125th Street.

I felt at home, making my way to Harlem to see it. Once, I even got my hair plaited into corn rows uptown, and I proudly sported my thick braids back downtown to ABT.

I was less enthusiastic about going to Brooklyn.

Why leave Manhattan? I wondered.

Leyla had to drag me there. On its own, even without its sister boroughs, Brooklyn would still be one of the biggest cities in the United States. It had its own distinctive flavor—from the West Indian restaurants standing cheek by jowl with Hasidic shops in Crown Heights to the stately brownstones in Park Slope. But Brooklyn never captured my heart the way Manhattan did. As we got older, Leyla began to prefer the more laid-back beer-garden vibe that she could find there. But I preferred the pumping beat that pulsated across the river.

Every weekend, on our days off, we'd hit another corner of the city. We'd shop along the cobblestoned streets of SoHo. Or we'd go to Central Park and stroll for hours. I would often go there by myself, throughout the summer, until the end of fall, listening to music and jotting down musings in my journal.

I loved that I could stand in line at the TKTS discount booth and grab a cheap ticket to nearly any Broadway show I wanted on my days off. I felt sophisticated and worldly wandering through art galleries and sculpture gardens.

I also loved the bohemian vibe of street fairs, ubiquitous in the city during the summer, especially on the Upper West Side. I would spend hours walking through, nibbling on shish kabobs or corn on the cob and drinking lemonade.

When I would go away for weeks at a time on tour with ABT, no matter how interesting or exotic the place we were visiting, I remember yearning to get back to "the city." I always felt like New York was moving and growing without me, and I was missing it all while I was away.

Turning twenty-one had opened up a whole other side of New York to me. I could hang out at luxurious all-night lounges and have the occasional glass of wine. Leyla and I went out dancing every weekend, and our favorite haunt, by far, was Lotus.

It was in the heart of New York City's meatpacking district. Once best known for transvestite prostitutes and butcher houses, the area's sticky cobblestoned streets still smelled of rotten meat. By the 2000s, the neighborhood transformed into the unlikely trendiest corner of Manhattan, and Lotus was its glittering beacon, filled every night with celebrities, young professionals, and all the cool kids. Leyla and I would go and dance until early morning. There were no *jetés* or *arabesques* in our moves, no worries about our "line" or technique. There was just sweaty, unbridled hip shaking, fueled by the giddiness we felt partying among the young and fabulous in New York City.

Looking so crazy in love's
Got me looking, got me looking so crazy in love

Someone tapped me on the shoulder.

"Mr. Diggs would like you to join him at his table."

Taye Diggs, the actor and star of *The Best Man* and *Private Practice* was sitting at a table in Lotus's VIP area. I walked over. It turned out he'd invited me so that I could meet his cousin, Olu, who was in New York working as a summer associate at a law firm.

Olu, caramel-skinned, gentle, and handsome, would become my first boyfriend. He said he'd had his eye on me all night. I later learned that he'd told Taye and his friends gathered around the table that one day I was going to be his wife.

We had to lean in close and murmur into each other's ear to be heard over the pounding beats of the music. Our connection was immediate. He was the son of a black father and Jewish mother, his ancestry mixed like mine. It was his last night in the city before returning to Atlanta, where he was attending Emory Law School. He had one year left to go.

I gave him my phone number, and over the next three months before he visited New York again, he and I talked on the phone and texted each other every day. That's the way it was for about a year—he'd come to the city every few months while we dated long distance, then he finally moved to Manhattan to start practicing as an attorney.

Olu had been raised a pescetarian, eating no meat—only fish. He worked out and was in wonderful shape, but he wasn't obsessive about weight or appearance. When we began dating, I relayed to him my frustrations, my fears. He was very subtle, and he chose the right words to guide and encourage me.

He made it all seem so easy. "Eat fish tonight instead of beef," he'd say. "Try cardio, but cut down on the resistance." He showed me that I just had to change a little here, a little there, to get back to where I wanted to be.

"ABT is still excited about you," he reassured me. "They still see a future with you. You just have to work on this one little thing."

I knew he thought I was beautiful, in any case. My weight no longer felt so overwhelming.

Olu had a countenance and confidence that I so admired and which, except for when I was onstage, I did not see an inkling of in myself. He made it his mission to change that, to help me learn to communicate through more than just dance. It was Olu who helped me realize that I did not need to run away from ABT to join Dance Theatre of Harlem. He truly believed that I had the talent to attain what I truly wanted, to become a soloist and principal right where I was. But I had to learn to ask for it.

I was very nervous about speaking up for myself. I didn't want to displease others, to be rejected or misunderstood. It seemed that whenever my voice had the courage to rise up—when I lived with Cindy, when I joined ABT's Studio Company—it would recede back to a hush at the first sign of adversity.

But Olu told me that I had to approach things in a different way, that I couldn't just feel sorry for myself: I had to fight. There's an old adage in the black community that we have to be ten times better just to get as much. I took that to heart. I had to be undeniably excellent. But I also had to let ABT know what I was after.

My boyfriend, ever the lawyer, decided that we should rehearse my argument. Our practices took place in his small Upper East Side apartment. He was a good taskmaster: he would give me time to pull my thoughts together, to jot down notes and bullet points on the topics that I wanted to cover. And then he'd enter the room and pretend to be Kevin.

"I want to be pushed," I'd read from my note card, my lips trembling. "I want to be a classical dancer. I'm a strong member of the company and can play those roles. And I want to give everything to this company. I appreciate the opportunity you've given me, and I want you to trust me, to believe in me."

"But you're so wonderful with the contemporary works," Olu would say, playacting as Kevin. "You shone in *Gong*. We have modern choreographers who want to create works just for you. Why not focus on those?"

"I know contemporary is a strength of mine," I'd say, my voice growing stronger, "But I want to be a *ballerina*."

It was terribly hard at first. I struggled to find my words, to express myself without reading them from a piece of paper. And I didn't want to disappoint Olu or to show him this embarrassing weakness.

Looking back, I also think that it was frightening for me to free my emotions. Few things elicited passion from me like ballet, and I think that I unconsciously feared that talking about how much ballet meant to me, how much I *needed* it, might break down my emotional dam and force to light other things with the power to cause me pain. Like the memories of my itinerant childhood; like my embarrassment that Mommy had had so many boyfriends and husbands; like the buried trauma that still lingered from my forced separation from Cindy.

But Olu was patient, supportive.

"You can do this," he'd say gently. "They picked *you*. Just remind them of all you can do."

As rehearsals usually go, whether for a meeting with your company's artistic director or a performance of *Swan Lake*, they helped to give me confidence, to drain away the tears and tension and leave behind what I needed to succeed.

I'd also started to realize that, despite my impatience, ABT *had* recognized my gifts. The fact that I was there at all, dancing with this illustrious company, was an opportunity that was one in a million. And when I looked at the big picture, it genuinely frightened me to think there might not be another woman of color in my position for a very long time.

Slowly, the fog that dampened my confidence began to lift. I made an appointment to talk to Kevin.

I could go days without seeing him. An executive as well as a creative director, Kevin was consumed with handling the business of ABT, and he was often in back-to-back meetings. Still, he would oversee some of the principal role rehearsals, as well as some run-throughs by the full company as we edged closer to premieres. Occasionally, I would have private rehearsals with Kevin if I was preparing for a starring role.

Otherwise, he was elusive, a shadow who all of us dancers knew was there, keenly watching every single performance.

I went to Kevin's office. It was finally time for me to speak.

"I know contemporary ballet is a strength of mine because a lot of ballerinas don't move like I do," I told him. "But I was trained as a classical dancer, and that's what I really want to do."

"I'm glad to hear that," Kevin said. "You have the talent to do both."

That was it.

Soon after, there was a new beginning. And I began to gain perspective.

Those first months in the corps I had been overwhelmed, not just by the dramatic changes in my body, or the occasionally negative reactions to my skin color, but by the competition I felt among my colleagues and friends.

But, I now realized, Kevin had pulled out a figurative ladder and was giving me opportunity after opportunity to pull myself up toward that prize I wanted so much to grab.

The role of an artistic director is complex. They are creative forces and also business executives. They have to be open, willing to take chances for the company to grow, yet stay true to the company's history and what it represents. They must make decisions about which dancers are capable of carrying the company and filling the theater's seats, while also entering the studio and giving each dancer the motivation that he or she needs to grow.

Kevin might have to dismiss a dancer at a moment's notice. He could give praise for a performance one day, then offer sharp criticism the next to ready someone for an upcoming show.

It was also true that he had watched me grow up, and with that our relationship evolved. I saw him at first as an authority figure, for whom I had tremendous respect and who I desperately wanted to please. He then became a mentor offering guidance and encouragement. And now, more than a decade later, I view him as a colleague to whom I can speak, grown-up to grown-up, dancer to dancer.

Recently, when I was on tour in L.A., I realized how far Kevin and I have come as I've grown up in ABT. It was the first time I felt that we could appreciate each other as adults. I had no idea how to communicate with a director as a nineteen-year-old—I spent most of my meetings with him as a teenager trying not to cry! My confidence developed slowly. I know he has an emotional connection to me, which I so value, just as he does with all of his dancers. It's part of what makes him so excellent and what makes ABT feel like a family. He always wants the best for us, though it's part of his job to criticize even his best-loved dancers, or in the worst cases, let them go.

One of the rituals I've treasured the most at ABT is the time just after the curtains close on our performances. Kevin watches all of our shows from a box at our theater, along with the other ballet masters and mistresses. If you watch closely about ten minutes before our last bows, you can see them slip away from their plush seats to escape backstage before the hallways of the Metropolitan Opera are thronged with patrons. Once the applause has died away, it's nearly eleven, and we're all exhausted—most nights, I just want to take off my makeup, go home, eat, and pass out before I have to wipe the sleep from my eyes at eight the next morning for class at ten. But by the time the curtain swings shut, Kevin is already on the stage with notes: "This is what you did wrong during the coda," he'll say, pointing to one of our principals. "For the next show, make sure you enter a beat sooner," he'll critique another. There's so much that needs to be said to all of us, and so little time between our shows during the hectic performance season that there's no time for sugarcoated niceties. Of course, he can't pay attention to all eighty dancers and what we're doing at every moment during a crowded company scene, but I'm constantly amazed by his and the artistic staffs' abilities to cut straight to the important corrections we need to be the best possible artists. It's an important postshow ritual for all of us, and when the season's over, I find myself craving that connection, that striving, that time to focus on my performance. It's comforting to know that, as busy as Kevin is with every other commitment he has as our artistic director, he'll always be there.

I look back and see that every step of the way, he has nurtured me, continuing to see my gifts and potential, no matter the ups and downs.

IN 2002, FOR INSTANCE, only a few months after I'd healed from my back injury and returned to the company, Kevin decided that he was going to have me represent ABT in one of the dance world's most prestigious competitions.

The Princess Grace Foundation awards scholarships and apprenticeships to the best young talents in dance, cinema, and theater. Every year, Kevin nominated one young dancer to compete for the honor. And that year, Kevin chose me.

Coming so soon after my year away, my being picked to be the face of ABT was like the bouquets leading ballerinas receive at the close of each performance: an offering to let me know how much Kevin and the company still believed in me. And it was also a chance to hop back on the proverbial horse, to not waste time fretting about having spent so much time away from ballet because I was now undeniably back in action.

I rehearsed with Kevin in preparation for the competition for a month. I would dance George Balanchine's famous *Tarantella*. Its *pas de deux* is exuberant, fun, and flirtatious. Balanchine created it in 1964 for Edward Villella, a principal dancer with New York City Ballet.

I got to partner with an old friend, Craig Salstein. He was my very first partner at ABT's summer intensive program, and then we moved on to the Studio Company together. He joined the main company a year after me, and we danced our very first peasant *pas de deux* from the ballet *Giselle*—with each other as corps members.

Having grown up in Miami, Craig was well acquainted with Edward Villella, the dancer for whom Balanchine created *Tarantella* and who eventually became the artistic director for Miami City Ballet. Craig worked directly with Edward for most of his training. He eventually became a soloist with ABT, like me.

Tarantella was, like its creator Balanchine, dazzling and quirky. It pushed the boundaries of the classical ballet world. It was full of contradictions, from big *grands jetés* to quick pointe work. I did a ton of *échappés,* rapidly moving my feet from a closed fifth position to an open second, as well as many steps that probably looked comical to an audience not familiar with ballet. I would start an *échappé, en pointe,* with my feet splayed, pointing in opposite directions, in second position. Then I'd *plié* again, still *en pointe,* tilting my head slightly to the side. It was an off-balance and fun effect you would usually never see in a stylized classical ballet. Craig and I each carried a tambourine that we used to shake and tap our hands and toes.

I also prepared one of the flower girl variations from *Don Quixote.* As a ballerina, it is hard to choose a ballet that is your favorite. It would be like saying that you prefer one child over another. You may indeed feel more in tune with your son than your daughter, but it feels like a betrayal, an insult to the other, to utter that affection out loud. Still, I must say that *Don Quixote* has always held a special place in my heart. It was the first full-length ballet I'd ever performed when I was attending Cindy's school. A variation from *Don Quixote* launched me after I performed it and won the L.A. Spotlight Award. And now, here it was again, for me to dance for the Princess Grace prize.

ABT filmed my two performances, and I gave them everything I had. We then sent the videotape to the Princess Grace Foundation for judging.

I didn't win. But I still felt victorious. I had achieved another milestone by competing, and I'd reinforced Kevin's faith in me.

BALLET WAS NEVER SOMETHING that was outside myself. As Misty the woman evolved and matured, so did my dancing.

Maybe it was because of the confidence I gained knowing I could heal from being hurt. Perhaps it was the realization that the timid girl from San Pedro could thrive on her own, in the urban melee of New York City. Or maybe it was knowing that I could be bent low by the occasional spectator deriding my caramel-colored presence, but rise again, undeterred, and stand my ground.

Whatever the motivations, all I know is that one day I woke up and made one of the most important emotional decisions of my life. I wanted to meet my father.

I had never ached for him. I had had Harold from the time I could remember, and he had been a loving, wonderful daddy to me in every way that he could possibly be, despite the flaws that had separated him from my mother. I had even had a relationship with Robert, though the way he treated my mother, my brothers, and especially my beloved baby sister, Lindsey, soured my memories of him. But a curiosity about the man who had actually been my dad had recently begun to grow, and now I was ready to take action.

Growing up, we had only the vaguest notions of why Mommy had picked up one day—Doug Jr., Chris, Erica, and me in tow—and hopped a Greyhound for California. We knew Mommy said she'd been unhappy, and since picking up and leaving is what she constantly did, there was little reason to ponder what had propelled her the first time, or whether the reasons were any different from those behind all her other departures.

So Mommy never spoke about our father, and we never asked. I never even saw his picture.

Somehow I understood that it wasn't his choice not to be a part of our lives. Rather, we kids felt, perhaps intuitively, that Mommy did not want us to reach out to him. So we didn't. After all, we Copelands were a tribe, with Mommy at the center. We knew from the crumbs of stories that she would drop along the way that she'd had a rough childhood, a tough life. And we wanted to protect her.

But after Doug Jr. graduated from high school, he decided that he wanted to find the man for whom he was named.

Doug had always been independent. He'd also been someone deeply interested in his roots, both cultural and familial. The little boy who'd tracked down a tuft of natural cotton to try to experience what it might have been like for our ancestors to pick it wanted to meet the man without whom he wouldn't exist.

I was about sixteen then, enjoying being back home, in a comfortable apartment with Mommy. I loved my studies at the Lauridsen Ballet Centre—hanging out with new friends and giddy from my summers away, first in San Francisco and then New York. I had ballet on my mind.

"Misty," Doug Jr. told me one afternoon as we sat together in the kitchen, when he was home from college. "I found our father."

"Our father?" I asked him, confused. Harold was only a few miles away. What was he talking about?

"Yeah!" Doug continued excitedly. "He's living in Wisconsin. I tracked him down, and we've been talking on the phone. I'm going to get some money together and go see him."

It all clicked. "Oh," I said. "That's great!" I was happy that Doug was so elated. But I wasn't really that interested.

Of course, Mommy hadn't known about Doug's search. But now that he'd found our dad, Doug Jr. didn't keep it a secret. He was grown, after all, so I guess she accepted it begrudgingly. Eventually, Doug Jr. did go see our dad, and he returned with a stack of photos detailing all the years that we had missed.

Senior and Junior looked just alike, copper-skinned and sinewy. Our father had apparently been a great athlete when he was young, and we figured that's where Chris and Doug Jr. had gotten their talents on the basketball court and football field from. I also concluded that was where I'd inherited my body structure, so much more muscular than Mommy's lithe frame.

It was fun hearing my father's stories from Doug Jr. But the rest of us were too busy with our present lives to reclaim the one we'd lost with a man we'd hardly known. Erica was living with her high school sweetheart, and together they were raising my beautiful niece, Mariah. Chris was focused on his studies, preparing to go to law school. And I was living my dream of performing with ABT.

But after being in the corps for a couple of years, I began to wonder more about my dad. What did he sound like when he spoke? Had he missed us? What might he think of his daughter, the ballerina? Those questions crowded my journal, began to haunt me in dance classes and through the streets of the Upper West Side.

One day I picked up the phone and called Doug Jr.

"I want to meet our dad," I told him.

"Okay," Doug said. "Let's book the tickets."

And on August 20, 2004, I met my father.

Doug Jr. and I flew to Wisconsin one weekend while I was on a break from ABT, and we stayed for a week. While I was there, I also met my great-aunt and a few of my cousins.

We Copeland kids had enjoyed wonderful, raucous gatherings with Harold's family, and I had a host of surrogate relatives, from the Cantines, my godparents; to Bubby; and even Robert's mother, Grandma Marie.

But I realized, when I breathed in the fragrance of my paternal grandfather's sister for the first time, that there was nothing like actually knowing an elder who shared the same blood. Mommy had been adopted and largely raised herself. So this was the closest I would ever get to an actual grandparent, to relatives whose ancestry was the same as mine.

My father was sweet. He was almost shy when he first greeted me, and then he wrapped me in his arms.

He was full of stories about his childhood in Kansas City, about being the son of a German mother and African American father. He told me how pretty Mommy had been when they met, how much he had cared for her, and how proud he had been of his four beautiful children.

It was crazy to me that he had been a phone call or plane ride away all this time and I had never seen him. Crazy—and also sad. But I was elated that I had made the effort to follow my curiosity where it led me, into my father's embrace.

"I have his lips," I jotted excitedly in my diary. "I wish I had his pretty hazel eyes. That would look fresh on me."

"It's like a part of me has been fulfilled. I'm really happy."

Of all the emotions I felt after meeting my father, anger at Mommy wasn't one of them. I think becoming a woman, and having to face and make my own difficult decisions, has helped me to understand her better. I knew that Mommy often handled difficulty by choosing not to deal with it.

I also understood that I was different from her, as was Doug, perhaps more so than our other siblings. We were reflective. We didn't want to flee. We wanted to take the situation and turn it over in our hands, to gaze at it and try to figure out how to make it better.

I thought of the trips I had taken: to China as an apprentice with ABT, to Mexico and Jamaica on my first cruise with Leyla, to Cape Cod with the Studio Company. And I thought that I would have given up every one of them to be here in Wisconsin, spending time with my father.

It was a joyful time, but Dad also spoke about more painful things. He had a long-time girlfriend, Debbie, whom he'd dated pretty much from the time my mother left him. But he never had any more children. He told my brother that he already had two sons and two daughters far away, and he never wanted any more. I know that he always loved us and wanted us to have a relationship. Our mother's leaving and our disappearing had taken a toll on him.

I had actually been startled when I first saw him. Compared to his pictures, he seemed shrunken, and his hair was turning gray. His hazel eyes sparkled, but he barely resembled the youthful man I'd seen in those photographs. Doug Jr. was a reflection of what our father had once been physically, but was no longer.

Though our growing happened without him, I think he is as proud as I am at how we all turned out. I marvel that I not only came through my chaotic childhood and somehow emerged as a professional ballerina, but that all my brothers and sisters have also done well.

To this day, I don't really understand how we did it, given the situations that we were put in. We'd been taken from our natural father, in the case of myself and my older siblings, and then from Harold, the only dad we'd ever truly known, to live with a man who spewed epithets. Next we lived with family friends in a gang-infested neighborhood, moved in with strangers, and then, finally, settled down in a shabby motel. It is still a wonder to me that not one of us has ended up in jail or on drugs.

Instead, we thrived. Chris eventually joined me in New York, and not long ago he passed the New York bar. Doug married his high school sweetheart, a beautiful woman whom I love like a sister. She is a physician, and Doug works in the insurance industry. They still live in California, where they are raising my adorable nephew.

I think Erica in many ways had it rougher than the rest of us, being the oldest and, in many ways, our surrogate mother. But she also has a great life. She's still strong, confident, and independent, and she and Mariah's father, Jeff, have been a couple for more than twenty years, ever since they were teenagers and he would give me rides to Cindy's school way across town.

Then there's Lindsey, who was a track star and attended Chico State University on a scholarship. She married a wonderful young man, and I was maid of honor at her wedding. Cameron, our youngest brother, is the most like me artistically. He was never much of an athlete, like Chris and Doug; instead, he's a prodigy at the piano. He still plays, and he also acts, sings, and writes music.

I rarely get angry when I think about my childhood, wishing for what we could have been if we'd had more of a nurturing home environment. It made us all strong fighters, primed to push through the toughest of struggles. But I do get frustrated with people who experienced relatively ideal lives and yet don't appreciate what they've had. Performing with ABT, I have sometimes overheard my dance mates complaining about going to the same vacation spot with their families, going on and on about how they'd rather be sunbathing than rehearsing, or how bad we have it at ABT versus City Ballet, or some other inconsequential thing.

I would think about all that I had been through, what I had to navigate and overcome to stand on the stage at the Metropolitan Opera. *What are these people fussing about?* I'd chuckle to myself. I do what I love for a living; I have my art, spend most of my time devoted to it, and travel the world while most can only dream of this opportunity. When our idyllic life at ABT is gone and we can no longer perform, I can guarantee that every one of those dancers will regret not appreciating every second of it while it was theirs.

Knowing what I'd survived, what all my siblings had made it through, makes me all the more grateful.

❦

A DECADE LATER, I feel as if I'm still struggling to get to know my dad, to do the impossible and recover all that lost time. But we are not giving up. Since Dad and Debbie live in Wisconsin, they often make the trek to Chicago whenever ABT performs there.

209

❦

Life in Motion

And every single Sunday when the phone rings at ten in the morning, it's my father on the line.

⚮

I DON'T KNOW IF meeting my father, holding my great-aunt's hand, and connecting with a previously undiscovered part of myself sparked something extra inside me. But I know that I returned to ABT from that trip to Wisconsin turbocharged. I felt incredibly motivated and excited, the way I had when I first went to Cindy's studio, looked in that wall of mirrors, and felt a jolt of recognition that I was finally where I was always supposed to be.

That soloist contract suddenly loomed large in my consciousness. It was no longer an elusive mirage but close enough to touch. And I didn't just want it for myself. Knowing that I could make history and be the first black female soloist with ABT in nearly twenty years made me so excited, I felt dizzy. I'd *said* it was my goal for years; that was one thing. But I was really starting to feel inside that it was truly possible. The expectation buoyed me.

"If this could open doors for black women in ballet, that would mean the world to me," I wrote in my ever-present journal. "It would all be worth it. That's what I'm doing this for. Not just for my own pleasure and gratification. I need to remember this every morning I wake up tired, just think[ing] of what I could do, not just for me but [for] others."

I was determined to focus like a laser on my technique and my performances over the next year. I would ultimately spend six years in the corps, and while I sometimes felt that I wasn't getting my due fast enough, I came to realize that many, indeed most members, never become soloists, the featured performer only a step away from being a principal. I would get that chance.

❦

ABT AND NEW YORK City gave me many gifts. The genesis of one remains a mystery.

Since I was seven years old, and my family left Harold to move in with Robert, I had suffered from crippling migraine headaches. I took medication to try to control them. I had missed my sweet sixteen party at the Lauridsen Ballet Centre because of a migraine, when I had to lie down in a dark room while the festivities went on without me. And they were so painful, I would often have to stumble to bed, sick to my stomach and barely able to see.

When I moved to New York, I was terrified those headaches would prevent me from performing and rehearsing.

But after a year with the Studio Company, I discovered that my migraines disappeared. My stress was different. I was different. I was in control.

I haven't had a migraine since.

Chapter 11

212

BESIDES KEVIN, THERE WERE other artists who gave me guidance and support. Like Isabel Brown. Hers is not a soft love. She is opinionated and gives praise only if it has been well earned.

The first time I performed with the Studio Company in New York City, she made sure to attend. Later that night, back at her Upper West Side brownstone, she came to my room with roses. I wondered why she had not presented them to me at the theater, where some of the other dancers had been greeted by parents and friends.

She set the vase on a side table.

"I didn't order the flowers until I saw that you'd performed well enough to deserve them," she said, giving me a cool stare.

That's Isabel, but I love her. I appreciate her generosity in allowing me to stay in her home, and her honesty, which let me know that if Isabel Brown said I was talented, then it was the truth. Isabel and her daughter Leslie, who taught some of my classes at ABT, watched my performances like hawks and gave me great praise, making me feel as if I was a member of their own illustrious family. After I joined the corps, Leslie was quoted as saying that I was one of the greatest young talents in ABT's main company. To have the stamp of approval from the Brown Dynasty is like being told you have a great voice by Pavarotti, or being feted by the Williams sisters for your powerful backhand.

I was also inspired and encouraged by another performer who had soared to the pinnacle of his art form, far from ballet. Prince.

✄

MY FRIEND KAYLEN RATTO, whom I'd met at the Lauridsen Ballet Centre and with whom I eventually went into business, was working for a company called Career Transition for Dancers, which helped ballerinas apply their discipline and skills to new professions once they're retired.

One Saturday morning, I woke up to a text.

"Can I give Prince your cell number?" it read.

Prince?

One of Prince's assistants had apparently called Kaylen's office, asking if someone there could track down my contact information. I didn't have a clue as to why Prince wanted to talk to me, but I told Kaylen she should definitely pass on my number.

Later that day, my cell phone rang.

Of course his speaking voice, a seductive baritone, bore little resemblance to the chandelier-shattering falsetto that he often summoned for his biggest hits. Still, it was impossible not to recognize who was speaking.

It sounds unreal, but I didn't particularly feel any way when he called. More than anything, I was intensely curious as to what he wanted.

I wasn't exactly his biggest fan. Boy bands, rappers, and R & B chanteuses were more my musical speed, but I knew his music from the radio and MTV. And, of course, I'd seen *Purple Rain*.

He spoke softly. "I'm remaking a song, 'Crimson and Clover,' and I would love to have you in the video."

I immediately zoned out, trying to envision how I would move to his music as a ballerina. The thought was odd but thrilling.

"That would be *awesome*," I said.

I sent an e-mail to Olu, who was out of town, telling him of the offer. I also called Mommy, who was even more excited than I was. Both thought I had to jump at the chance.

ABT was on hiatus, so I could essentially do whatever I wanted. Prince and I figured out a date that worked, and a few days later I was on my way to Los Angeles. I flew first class. And though my family lived there, Prince had booked me a room at the Beverly Hills Hotel—an unbelievably plush suite, far too big for one person. Flowers, champagne, and a hand-written note were there in the room to welcome me. Prince's assistant was in charge of taking me to and from the studio where we shot the video. Otherwise, I was ferried around in a limousine.

I was sitting in the makeup chair at the video shoot the next day when Prince finally walked in. He was carrying an adorned cane. But he was very quiet and humble, not at all what I guess you'd expect from a superstar. He casually walked over, said hello, and shook my hand. He seemed almost nervous.

I was to be my own choreographer, improvising to the music. He respected that I knew my art form far better than he did. On the set he sat quietly, just watching, allowing me to discover and create in the moment.

That evening, the limousine came to pick me up and take me to Prince's home for dinner. When I got in, I found a lavishly wrapped gift. Inside the box was the sand-colored couture gown that I'd worn on set during the video shoot.

A member of Prince's staff let me into his house. I must have waited forty-five minutes in a living room area opposite the kitchen, making small talk with his chef while I watched anxiously for him to arrive. I peered around his beautiful home. There were windows everywhere, stretching from floor to ceiling, and they provided a moonlit frame to his sexy, purple piano.

Finally, I could hear his heels clicking down the hallway as he came to get me. He walked me to the dining room, where we sat and ate the vegan meal his chef had prepared. It was an unbelievably long table. He sat at the head of it, and I sat beside him.

From the beginning he showed an enormous amount of admiration and interest in learning everything there was to know about me and ballet. He asked a ton of questions about my background, what music I enjoyed, how I felt performing, and what my experience had been at ABT.

After dinner the limousine carried me back to the hotel. And I wouldn't see Prince again for another year.

He would call me every so often. One day he invited me

to see the funk rock group Graham Central Station perform in New York City. Once again he sent a car. Once again he was shy. We sat at a large round table, just the two of us. At one point during the evening he got onstage to play the guitar. He was masterful, fierce, and passionate, and he drove the audience crazy. It was the first time I saw that side of him. Then the night was over. I went home.

That's the way it was with Prince. He would disappear, and then just pop back into my life, out of the blue. It was mysterious but also exciting. About five months later, he called again.

"I'm going on tour in Europe," he said. "I'd love for you to be a part of some of the shows. You could maybe even kick it off with a solo."

While it was easy for me to work with Prince while ABT was on hiatus, if I wanted to do something outside the company during rehearsal or performance season, it was much more difficult. I would have to request a release, and I would likely be docked in pay. Most such requests are denied.

I would just barely make the deadline in the end: the European tour would take place later in the summer, so I was free to go.

It was an unimaginable opportunity. Not only would I be able to work with a pop icon, I'd present ballet to a whole new audience. *This is unreal,* I thought. But I played it cooler than that.

"I think I can come," I said calmly.

When I arrived at Paris's Charles de Gaulle Airport, Prince was waiting for me in a black Town Car. We didn't speak much on the ride to the hotel. We stayed at the Hôtel Le Bristol, where I ran into the actress Rachel McAdams while I was waiting for Prince outside his room. She was in the midst of shooting the film *Midnight in Paris.*

That first evening, Prince and I went to see the singer Erykah Badu. Her performance was like an act of communion. She was ethereal, sensual, and clearly having the time of her life.

Later that evening, Erykah sat with me to watch Prince perform in a jam session at an after-party. The night was endless. Prince must have played for four hours straight—that's how much he loved his art. He could compose and rehearse it all day, then play at it all night. As a dancer, I completely understood that passion.

We were supposed to have a show in Paris, but it ended up being canceled. I don't recall why. I'm sure there was a dramatic write-up about it and possibly a lawsuit involved, which happens with such things. At any rate, we ended up only doing one show, in Nice, France.

We arrived in Cannes a couple days later. The band and crew stayed at the Negresco Hotel, but Prince was very particular about his accommodations and didn't feel comfortable there. The two of us drove around, finally settling in at the Grand Hyatt Cannes Hôtel Martinez instead. It was quite the drama, trying to find a place at the last minute. But this was Prince after all. He made it happen.

When it was time finally to do our show, we went to the venue and were shown the dressing room. Prince and I had to share, something that he apologized for, and something I later learned rarely happens to such a superstar. But I was fine with it. We sat and talked, joking around as we applied our makeup.

After Prince's band and background singers made their way onto the stage, I was next. I walked out, not really knowing what I was going to do since I hadn't rehearsed. But I wasn't worried. I was in the zone. I was about to perform, which I loved to do, but far away from ABT, so I didn't have to worry about executing the perfect forward leap, or *jeté en avant*, with all eyes critiquing my form. I could dance freely and introduce some newcomers to my love, ballet.

I had been dancing for about a minute or two—raising my leg at the hip, with my knee nearly touching my forehead, lowering it sharply, knees straight, a *grand battement*—when the crowd erupted into screams and cheers.

Wow, I thought, feeling a charge. *They liked that!*

Then, as I spun around, I caught a glimpse of Prince walking onto the stage. The roar, of course, had been for him. I chuckled to myself and slowly exited the stage. I stood there in the wings, taking it all in. It was the first time I saw my new, easygoing, curious friend as *Prince*, the legendary musician. I actually stood there with my mouth open, awestruck by his transformation. He was kinetic and yet totally in control. And his fans were as passionate for him as he was for them. It was the type of artistry and connection with the audience that I sought to emulate in my own career.

PRINCE DISAPPEARED AGAIN FOR maybe another year before suddenly calling me once more in the fall of 2011. He wanted to fly me to his home in Minnesota for a photo shoot and to discuss a new collaboration. I agreed, and just as before, I went to see him, not really knowing much about what he wanted.

He told me that he was planning to tour the States, something he hadn't done in a very long time. The tour would be called Welcome to America and would kick off with a concert in New York City at Madison Square Garden. I was honored that he wanted me to be involved, especially in the tour's beginning stages, when he was envisioning and charting the tour's look and flow.

We did a photo shoot together, him with his guitar and me in the gown and pointe shoes I'd worn nearly two years earlier in the "Crimson and Clover" video. I *pirouetted* and posed around him while he focused solely on the camera. A couple of hours later, when we were done, I went to another room in his home to sit with some of his staff, who were ready to pick the pictures that we'd use. I did the choosing, selecting those that best showed my dancer's lines since they didn't have the eye for that uniquely balletic attribute. They accepted that I knew best and then printed the shots that would be used in the posters and programs that would be on sale during the shows.

Playtime, however, was over. There would be no more improvising onstage. This time, Prince wanted a choreographed and set piece.

❧

WHEN I RETURNED TO New York, ABT was in full swing preparing for our *Nutcracker* season at the Brooklyn Academy of Music. We were using a theater space in New Jersey for our daily rehearsals since the BAM facility would be occupied by another company until our premiere.

I would rehearse with ABT from about ten in the morning

until nine at night. Then, during my breaks, I had a choreographer meeting me at the theater to work on the number I would do during Prince's concert. I would be dancing to "The Beautiful Ones" from Prince's movie and album *Purple Rain*.

After rehearsing all day and half the night with ABT, I was picked up from the theater in a limousine to go to the Izod Center in New Jersey, where I would then rehearse with Prince until about two in the morning. He was now very particular about what he wanted from me. But I was comfortable with that. This was the type of high-pressure environment I was used to as a ballerina, and while it had been fun to do what I'd wanted in the shows before, it was comforting to strive again for technical perfection and control. I was ready.

Prince would write pages of notes for me and the choreographer. He would have me listen to the "Beautiful Ones" over and over again until I knew every word and musical cue.

Baby, baby, baby,
What's it gonna be?

Sometimes we would rehearse in his suite at the Ritz-Carlton in Manhattan, and he would blast the music as I danced on the dining room table, our substitute for the piano that I would whirl atop onstage during the concerts.

Working with Prince—experiencing his brilliance, his attention to detail, but also his belief in me—boosted my confidence immeasurably. Executing something that was his vision but based largely on my own, without the incremental coaching of my ballet mistresses, made me feel independent, as if I was truly a professional at last.

Up to that point, I'd still often felt like a student, the perennial latecomer to ballet. Working with Prince helped me to become a whole artist, responsible for every step I danced from its conception to its execution, from its birth to its final flourish.

❧

MY EMOTIONAL BREAKTHROUGHS—MEETING AND falling in love with Olu, learning to cherish my new body, meeting my father for the first time—seemed to flow alongside technical breakthroughs in my dancing.

I remember the first time I performed George Balanchine's *Tchaikovsky Pas de Deux* at the Met with Jared Matthews. It was in May 2009, and it was a significant turning point for me. Quick footwork, especially in Balanchine ballets, was always a challenge for me. I practiced relentlessly and performed well, a major accomplishment. And my technique improved each time I performed.

I have found that most of my progression and break-throughs came when I was asked to perform outside of ABT. I think that was because in those outside shows, I was always the principal dancer, and I was able to perform major parts without the expectations and pressure I felt from ABT's staff.

Sometimes the pressure existed solely in my own head. There was always the fear that if I had an off day, if I could not maintain the illusion of perfection that we dancers endlessly sought but could not attain, I would never be cast in that part again. But dancing outside of ABT, I felt as if there was less to lose. Worry and tension was replaced by pure, unfettered joy.

I didn't just experience that burst of confidence and adrenaline dancing with other companies or choreographers. I felt the same freedom and electricity performing with Prince.

He was a perfectionist, like me, and he wanted to see certain elements in my performance. Still, I was the expert on ballet, and so it was up to me to choreograph, hone, and then perform my piece, all on my own.

He and I would stare at the mirror, figuring out poses that worked for me to do around him as he sang "The Beautiful Ones" on his U.S. tour. I would not be at every concert. Since ABT was in the midst of its season at the Brooklyn Academy of Music, I'd gotten permission to perform with Prince on our off nights, and Prince was fine with my coming and going according to my schedule with ABT, cutting my piece on the nights I was on at BAM.

I was exhausted and exhilarated. I've performed all over the world, from the Metropolitan Opera to the Karl Marx Theatre in Havana and the Cultural Centre in Hong Kong, but performing with Prince was something I could never have prepared for.

The first show was at Madison Square Garden, and I felt a bit more pressure than usual. The audience was filled with celebrities, and the air was crackling with intensity.

During the show, I sneaked under the stage, where Prince had a small changing room. He would perform a couple of songs before coming to join me. When he came downstairs, we were quiet. Then we hugged.

"Let's do it," he said.

Then he stepped onto a small square platform that rose from beneath the stage. He walked to the piano and started playing.

The platform was supposed to lower again for me to step on, rise, and take my place alongside Prince.

But the stage wouldn't lower.

I began to panic. *Oh no*, I thought. *That's my cue! I'm supposed to be onstage!*

It seemed to take minutes, but after a few seconds, the platform dropped to meet me.

I gracefully walked to the piano and picked up where I needed to. Prince's relentless drills to make sure that I knew every lyric, every chord, helped me find my place without missing a beat. I felt ebullient.

I was about to have my solo when Prince stopped singing.

"Ladies and gentlemen, Misty Copeland!" My heart started pounding. He'd never done that in any rehearsals. I always saw myself as the backup dancer, twirling in the background. Now he'd introduced me to his audience, as if I were his equal, his partner. I was floating.

To be truthful, I don't believe that I was able really to showcase what I was capable of as a ballerina. The gown—the same one I'd worn years before in the "Crimson and Clover" video and that Prince insisted I wear during his concerts—was a size four. I was barely a size zero. And its train was too heavy and long to allow me to execute jumps or intricate turns. Even the stage wasn't quite right, with flooring that wasn't appropriate for dancing in pointe shoes.

For the most part, I walked around in a very sultry way, doing *piqué* turn after *piqué* turn, going into a string of *chaînés* until I could no longer keep from becoming dizzy with the added weight of my dress's long train. Still, it was nothing too technically difficult. My greatest balancing act was making sure I didn't slip off as I spun on top of the piano.

Still, I'll never, ever forget it. I was performing in concert arenas, giving a taste of ballet to many who had never seen one. Prince and I would do several more shows together at Madison Square Garden, and at the Forum in Los Angeles, and it was an experience that is incomparable.

Prince loved watching the ballet, and came to ABT to see my performances often. He gave me confidence I hadn't felt since I was a young dancer. One of the things I most value about our friendship was that he helped me realize my worth at ABT. I didn't need to be so humble all the time, he said, just as Mr. Mitchell tried to tell me. You are a queen, a diva in the best way, he'd say. I felt like a different person onstage knowing that someone as talented as he is had confidence in me. As fleeting as his presence in my life was, I know I will be forever grateful for it.

It was also incredible that ABT was so generous, allowing me to take advantage of these other opportunities when there were times they could definitely have said no. And of course, they would express great support for my work inside the company, which was the most affirming of all.

I realized that support was there from the beginning. I frequently recalled those heady days during the first two summers I danced with ABT. I remember when Elaine Kudo, the wonderful dancer who had been the first to dance with Baryshnikov in Twyla Tharp's *Push Comes to Shove*, approached me one day. She had seen me perform the year before in a contemporary piece created by Kirk Peterson called *Eyes That Gently Touch*, and she wanted to tell me how beautiful she thought my performance had been. She said that she had seen two other professional companies perform the same piece, and mine was by far the best she had seen. I was honored beyond words.

I also recall David Richardson, ABT's then assistant artistic director, coming up to me one day and telling me that John Meehan had mentioned me the day before.

"I'm very excited about this coming season," David said John told him.

"Why?" David asked.

"Because there's going to be a Misty Copeland and a David Hallberg," John was quoted as saying, speaking of pieces featuring me and the brilliant young dancer who eventually became a principal with ABT. David said that John told him that I was very talented. I felt so validated, so appreciated, I could have achieved *ballon* and never come down.

Chapter 12

THE TECHNICAL BREAKTHROUGHS, THE chances to
dance with other companies and performers like Prince, and the
words and demonstrations of support from Kevin McKenzie
and others helped me to believe in my talent and to speak up
for myself, not just about dance, culture, and art—but about
race.

Knowing the footsteps of other black ballerinas who had
come before also helped me to find my voice.

My introduction to Raven Wilkinson came while watching
a documentary on the Ballet Russe. It was the first time I'd ever
heard of her, which made me angry and happy at the same time.
I was enraged that neither I, a young ballerina, nor many of my
peers, had ever heard of Raven, yet I was overjoyed that I had
finally found her.

When the Ballet Russe toured the South, Raven had con-
tended with the Ku Klux Klan's threats. Because of the whispers of racially tinged violence, she eventually had to leave the

company and move to Holland to find a home where she could dance again. I wept as I watched her story. But I also knew now that I was not alone as a black ballerina and had been fortunate to walk a far less treacherous path.

I spoke about Raven so often that my manager, Gilda Squire, decided to do some research. She discovered that Raven was still very much alive, living in an apartment only a couple of blocks away from me on the Upper West Side. I felt this was a sign that we were supposed to meet and be there for each other.

Gilda reached out to Raven and learned that she had followed my career from its onset, watching all of my TV interviews and reading many of the articles about me. I was moved and surprised.

Finally, Gilda set up an event at the Studio Museum in Harlem. It would be a public conversation between two generations of black ballerinas: Raven and me. The first time I ever spoke to Raven, we were not even in the same room. We participated in a live radio interview to promote the Studio Museum event, and I got very emotional, just hearing her voice. We finally met only a couple of minutes before we took the stage together for the conversation in Harlem. I burst into tears and hugged her tightly. She was so small, delicate, and beautiful.

We have stayed in touch ever since. She attends all of my performances, and we'll often go out afterward for a meal. Even before I was able to meet her, she had been a guiding light in my life, and now she constantly, selflessly encourages me to go further than she ever could. She often says I have so much more ability and talent than she did, which I find hard to believe. She is humble, hilarious, and so full of funny, poignant tales that she never repeats one. We speak the same very rare language: that of a black classical ballet dancer.

I think part of my purpose as an African American ballerina is to share Raven's story and educate people on our history within the ballet world. Not just Raven, but Aesha Ash, Alicia Graf Mack, Lauren Anderson, Tai Jimenez, and the myriad other black swans who have enriched the world of ballet but who have often not gotten their due. I feel a strong connection to them all. It isn't easy for us in this world. Ballet is still a career that requires either a lot of luck (which I had) or a lot of money (which I didn't have). In addition to impeccable training and emotional support. And as you climb, it can be lonely and terrifying to look around and see no one else who resembles you. Aesha, Tai, and especially Raven made me feel less alone.

IN A BALLET COMPANY, you often have to compete with your friends, your peers, for the same role. That's never easy. But to compete on an uneven playing field is even more psychologically exhausting.

I remember that awful, empty feeling in my gut when I walked into a rehearsal with a ballet mistress, knowing that she had already made up her mind about who I was and what I was capable of. I could always tell. Having to put on a face of confidence, knowing that I would most likely not be cast, no matter how well I performed, taxed me emotionally. As did feeling that I sometimes had to defend who I was.

"But we don't think of you as black" was the refrain from some of my peers when I made a small attempt to open up about my concerns that I had a harder time getting some classical roles, or getting recognition for some of my performances.

Of course they were trying to be nice, empathetic even. Instead, it just made me wonder, *Well, how do you see black people in general if you believe* not *thinking of me that way is a compliment?*

But I kept on dancing and practicing and performing. I got stronger in every way. And I can't describe how it feels when you finally get someone to focus on your talent and not the superficiality of the package you come in.

Three years ago, I was playing the part of Puss in Boots in *Sleeping Beauty.* The makeup person was standing at the ready with her container of powder to turn my face white.

I looked at her. "I don't understand why the cats have to be white," I said defiantly. "I want to be a brown cat."

And so I was.

❧

IN 2007, KEVIN McKENZIE nominated me to be one of two ABT dancers to represent the company in the famous Erik Bruhn Competition.

The artistic directors of the four top ballet companies in the world—ABT, the Royal Ballet, the Royal Danish Ballet, and the National Ballet of Canada—each select their top young dancers to take part.

I believe that Kevin has always thought I had something extra, and that's why he gave me every scholarship, fellowship, or workshop opportunity he could offer, from the Coca-Cola Scholarship that paid for my training my final year in Southern California to my selection to compete for the Princess Grace prize. And now this. He was giving me the chance to step up and become a principal on the stage.

My fellow corps member Jared Matthews and I would compete on ABT's behalf, with the hope of winning. I was relieved to have Jared, my friend and frequent *pas de deux* partner, by my side.

Three days before the competition in Canada, I hurt myself in rehearsal executing one of my jumps. I was preparing to dance the part of the jumping girl in *Swan Lake's pas de trois*, which I would perform on tour with ABT right after we returned from across the border. I was told that I had a stress reaction in my metatarsal. I was panicked and devastated, but determined to push through. I took the next day off, then returned to the ABT studios to see if I would be able to dance.

As I opened the door to the dressing room, I saw an unfamiliar suitcase sitting in the center of the room. No one had told me that another girl from the company was prepared to go in my place, but that was the message I received, startling and clear. I knew I had to pull it together. There was no way I was going to miss my chance. That night, despite the pain and nervousness I felt, I decided to go to Canada and compete.

There Jared and I danced the *Grand Pas de Deux* from *Sleeping Beauty* that I'd performed so many times with ABT's Studio Company. We also danced a contemporary piece, an excerpt from *Petite Mort*, choreographed by Jiří Kylián.

The other dancers from the other three companies were, surprisingly, friendly. I think we were all united knowing what an honor it was to be selected by our respective directors to compete, and also feeling the pressure of performing on such a grand stage. I was particularly anxious about our piece from

Sleeping Beauty. I think I was told so often at ABT that I excelled in more contemporary roles that I felt a little intimidated taking on such an iconic, classical part.

I gave my best performance yet that night. In the end, we lost the competition. But I won the greater prize.

A few weeks later, after I'd returned home, Kevin asked me to come see him.

He had decided, at last, to make me a soloist. Kevin told me that the night of the Erik Bruhn Competition was the first time he saw me as a true ballerina.

I would be the first black soloist with ABT in twenty years. It was a historic breakthrough.

But hearing his words, I felt surprisingly calm. It wasn't at all the way I had imagined it since the age of thirteen.

In that dream, I dropped to my knees in tears, thanking Kevin from the bottom of my heart. Now that it was real, after fighting so hard for so long, through years of doubt, I finally believed that I deserved this.

Still, I recognized then and now that Kevin had been behind me from the start, pushing me to grow, to mature, to excel. Giving me, so unlikely a ballerina, the chance to stand at center stage and be the face of one of the most distinguished dance companies in the world is something I will forever be grateful for.

I had waited six long years, and now I was ready, not just to show the world that I was a gifted dancer but that I was a true artist as well.

IN JUNE 2011, I would join the likes of Denzel Washington, Jennifer Lopez, Kerry Washington, Cuba Gooding Jr., Smokey Robinson, Magic Johnson, and Sugar Ray Leonard, among other accomplished Boys and Girls Clubs of America alumni, to participate in a PSA that would run as an inspirational commercial for the clubs.

As a ballerina, we don't often feel the benefits of a lifetime of hard work and determination put into our craft. But to come from such an organization, and to be surrounded by people who excel in their arts, and started out just like you, whom you look up to and then are recognized next to, is really cool. The cast mingled very casually, like we were old friends. I guess all being club kids, we felt connected. Denzel shared with me a great story. As a youngster in New York, he took any and every opportunity to be on or near a stage, so when the Metropolitan Opera House needed curtain boys, he jumped at the chance. He ended up pulling the curtain back for Natalia Makarova and Mikhail Baryshnikov in a production with ABT. Kerry expressed her interest in supporting me and ballet and was incredibly friendly.

In 2012, I traveled to San Diego to be inducted into the Boys and Girls Club Hall of Fame.

Liz and Dick Cantine were there, as well as my mother. And Cindy and Patrick were in attendance.

Beforehand, the staff at the Boys and Girls Club asked if I wanted to invite Cindy. I told them yes, absolutely. I'd seen the Bradleys here and there over the years.

But the Boys and Girls Club ceremony was the first time we'd all been together under one roof—Mommy, the Cantines, the Bradleys—since the ugly battle over my emancipation.

Cindy was among the many I thanked in my acceptance speech for bringing me to ballet. I don't think I'd ever really thanked her before. It was well deserved.

I was so proud that they were all there—Mommy, and Liz and Dick, and Patrick and Cindy—that we had overcome this huge trauma and could celebrate what had come before it and what had happened since. What a great thing, that I could be on this stage at the Boys and Girls Club, where I first touched the barre, and that they could all experience the triumph with me!

I felt so happy making that speech. I looked out at their beaming faces, and I wasn't nervous at all.

Chapter 13

WHEN I WAS A little girl, I lived in terror of being judged, of letting others down. I was the people pleaser. I diligently made sure everyone got to class on time when I was a hall monitor. I was the first to volunteer to run errands, to clean the table, to help my brothers and sisters.

When my brothers and sisters would grouse about Mommy's boyfriends, or even about Mommy herself, I would hold my tongue. I would rather sit in an empty hallway, listening to my own echo, than risk being late to class. And when I lived with Cindy and was still in public school, I'd make a tent with my bedspread and use a flashlight to study for tests late into the night.

Then I chose an unlikely path. I became a ballerina. And that meant being judged all the time.

With every rehearsal at ABT's studios, every performance at the Met or Brooklyn Academy of Music, I risked letting down everybody who believed in me, perhaps no one more so than myself.

I had countless people in my corner, from my mother, who loved me enough to let me leave her for a little while to live with the Bradleys, to Kevin McKenzie, who gave me my dream of dancing with ABT.

But there have, and continue to be, many in the ballet world who criticize me, whose twisted notions about my looks, my ability, and my motives hurt me still.

Some bloggers felt that my appearances with Prince demeaned ballet. Others decried the fact that I had the nerve to "play" the race card. Others cited the many articles about me as proof that I wasn't much more than a press-hungry amateur.

I wanted not to read these vitriolic words. And then, when curiosity wouldn't let me leave well enough alone, I wanted it not to hurt, not to make me angry. But it did both.

Paloma never reads her reviews, though she's in a small minority of dancers who are able to disconnect from the public in that way. For me, being active online and in social media is another way of connecting with my fans, whether they're the ones who have front-row subscriptions to ABT or have only seen clips of my dancing on a tablet screen. But there are people who will just never want to see me dance because of my race. No matter what I do or how I do it, they won't like me.

I'm tempted by Paloma's resolution: she doesn't have to deal with the comments that numb your artistry and tear your soul apart—she doesn't live in fear that the joy of doing what she loves will be taken from her. I never want that.

How do I explain what it is like for someone who has never met you, has never walked your path, to view you through a fractured lens and then render judgment? Giving interviews, dancing with Prince, and taking every opportunity I can to speak to young people are what I do *because* I love ballet, not to exploit it. I want to share this beautiful art form, which at its heart is so uplifting, with as many people possible because I know the joy and grace that it has given me.

I also find it interesting when people talk about my mixed roots. Most black people have ancestors who came from Europe or the indigenous groups of the Americas. My blackness has always been clear to those who want to say I do not fit into the classical world of ballet. But when I am getting media attention for beating the odds, and gaining unlikely success in this exclusive, cloistered world, suddenly my Italian and German grandmothers take center stage.

I choose to define myself. I am a black woman, and my identity is not a card to play, or a label that I begrudgingly accept because it's been assigned to me. It's the African American culture that has raised me, that has shaped my body and my worldview. Admittedly, I don't always handle my hurt and outrage at the prejudice I see so often very well, but I have agency in being able to speak my mind. So many times, I'll hear the seven-year-old girls I teach reflect the bigoted mentality that poisons the dance world. They're children and already have to deal with such grown-up messes. It's very much an issue. And while I want everyone who sees me dance to be transported and transfixed, when I soar across the stage, I feel that I am carrying every little brown girl with me, those with broken wings and those who are just about to take flight.

Someone once asked me if, as a dancer, I ever have a perfect night. Sometimes it seems that way. You feel totally in balance. You land every jump perfectly. Your arms float like ether, and your body arches strong and gracefully. Dancers say then that "you're on. You're on your leg."

But that is rare. Instead, I think a professional dancer is always striving to be able to correct what's askew, to make things work when they're off. We train our bodies to be able to find balance when we're off-kilter, and to quickly deal with whatever is thrown at us—a missed beat, a twisted ankle, a stumble or fall.

Before every rehearsal, without fail, I go to ballet class. And I always begin with a warm-up at the barre. I work at it like I'm back at the Boys and Girls Club in San Pedro, touching it for the first time. Some days, I stand on one leg and find that I am tired, that I am weak. So I shift my weight to find another way to stand tall and push through.

That has been my mental battle as well: to block out the criticism, to remember all the little brown girls who are counting on me. Then to stand tall. And push through.

❧

I WAS IN TOKYO, performing as a flower girl in *Don Quixote*, when I first heard about *The Firebird*.

It was in the fall of 2011, and I'd been a soloist for four years. With music composed by Igor Stravinsky, *The Firebird* is a work that melds the most virtuosic parts of ballet with bravura solos that tell a story of spells, mystical creatures, and love triumphing over evil.

As the story goes, Prince Ivan loses his way and winds up in an enchanted garden, where he comes upon and captures the beautiful Firebird. When she breaks away, she leaves behind a magic feather that he can use to call her if he is ever in trouble.

Next, the wandering prince encounters thirteen frolicking princesses. The young maidens are under a spell, cast by the sorcerer Kaschei. He wants to keep them all to himself. But Prince Ivan is smitten with one of the dancing maidens.

When Ivan clashes with the evil Kaschei, he waves the Firebird's magical feather. She appears and casts a spell of her own, forcing the wicked sorcerer and all who are gathered to dance themselves to exhaustion. The Firebird eventually guides the prince to an egg which holds Kaschei's soul. Ivan breaks it. Soon, the princesses are liberated from the deep, dark magic that had entranced them and the sorcerer's other victims are also freed. The magical garden blooms in sunshine once more and the Firebird triumphantly rises over the prince and his love, like an angel.

It is a beautiful, iconic role. One day, Kevin pulled me aside and told me that I would be learning the part.

That was unusual. Usually, there is a casting list, hanging on a board at ABT's headquarters where the dancers can see every role for every ballet the company is performing that year. Next to the roles are lists of names in the order of the cast in which they will appear. Your name being written there doesn't guarantee that you will be in the principal role. You might be preparing to be an understudy.

Three to four weeks before the first performance, that same board notes the dates that you will perform, and lets you know, finally, if you will perform as the principal. ABT will also issue press releases announcing who will play which roles, and when, during the season.

Kevin told me himself that I'd be learning Firebird. It was the most expedient way for me to find out, because I was going to have to commit to rehearsing for it during a company layoff.

I assumed I would be an understudy, but I was still thrilled to be studying Alexei Ratmansky's new choreography.

I dove into rehearsals, determined that if ever I needed to fill in for the lead, I would be ready.

Alexei challenged me with his eccentric, brilliant choreography. His steps were more contemporary than classical, and there was really no established vocabulary to describe them. *The Firebird* would have two big solos, as well as a *pas de deux*. The first solo was extremely important because it would form the first impression of this mythical creature, and Alexei was obsessed with getting it just right. Three casts would be performing the ballet, and the Firebird in each would have her own unique entrance.

For my entrance to the stage, Alexei wanted me to run out at full speed and then come to an abrupt stop while the musical score continued to play. Then he wanted the Firebird to execute a dramatic movement that demonstrated her power, her wildness. I was constantly focused on that as I looked in the mirror during rehearsals. Normally, in classical ballet you want to hold your neck in alignment with your spine. But as this wild creature, I jutted my chin forward.

What also made working with Alexei so special was that unlike so many choreographers who merely verbalized their vision, Alexei was able to demonstrate—an off-balance *piqué*, a jerky *pirouette*. My ability to immediately mimic whatever motion I saw was critical. And learning the steps in this visceral way was also refreshing. With many classical ballets created centuries ago, you don't really know what the creator intended. Instead, you're trying to interpret an assumption. Not so with Alexei's modern inventions.

Still, Alexei's vision was not easy to bring to life. He didn't want it to be. In *The Firebird*'s *pas de deux*, Prince Ivan is trying to capture the creature, and she is trying frantically, poignantly, to escape. It is a struggle, not a romantic embrace. Alexei's choreography reflected that.

At the same time I was learning the part of the Firebird, I was participating in a choreographic workshop with Dance Theatre of Harlem. The company had been resurrected after its long hiatus, and ABT was on a summer layoff for two months. The workshop would have no final performance. It was simply, beautifully, an exercise in creation, as expressed by myself, one other young woman, and two young men. It was an honor to participate in finding the identity for the new Dance Theatre of Harlem, under Virginia Johnson's direction. I also continued to find comfort there, surrounded by dancers who looked like me and who unconditionally supported, rather than questioned, my talent.

We had a busy morning of choreographing and improvising together. Finally, we got a five-minute break, and I plopped down on the floor, exhausted, and picked up my phone. I started browsing idly through Twitter as I stretched my tired legs.

And that's how I found out.

There was a link to an ABT press release about the official casting for *The Firebird*. Natalia Osipova, ABT's guest principal dancer, would be in the first cast.

And I—Misty Copeland—would be the Firebird in the second.

I would become the first black woman in history to play the Firebird for a major ballet company.

My eyes welled with tears. For a moment, I couldn't speak.

"Is everything okay?" someone asked with concern. "Is it your family?"

"No," I said. "I've been cast as the Firebird." Then I burst into tears.

Everyone around me started crying as well. There were arms everywhere as they reached out to grab me, hug me.

When you are in a dance company, the other members are like your family. Some of my dearest friends have been the boys and girls, men and women, whom I danced beside, whether in San Pedro, in San Francisco, and of course in New York City, within ABT.

Many of my peers at ABT later congratulated me, happy for my achievement. But I know, in the moment when I discovered that I had been cast, their reaction would not have been like what I received that day among the company members of Dance Theatre of Harlem.

Though I was not officially a member of their company, we were family because we shared a different, more profound bond. They were also black dancers, and they felt the significance of this moment in a way that few others would: deep within their souls. They knew, without my needing to spell it out, every setback or curve in the road: that I had fought for ten years to be recognized, to show that I had the talent and ability to dance in classical ballets. They had fought that fight alongside me. And so they felt as much pride and elation as I did, seeing an African American dancer cast in the lead role of such an iconic classical ballet.

As for me, my tears were as much an outpouring of relief as they were happiness. I was incredibly excited. But I also felt a weight that I had carried on my back for a decade slowly getting lighter.

I'm not sure that I could have rehearsed any more intensely than I already had been. I approached every ballet class like a rehearsal, every rehearsal as if it was an actual performance. I was immersed in the part completely, practicing up to seven hours a day, five or six days a week, for six months.

While I focused on the performance, ABT's historic decision was making waves. Numerous African American luminaries, from the worlds of television, literature, and the arts, were purchasing tickets to my premiere. My mentors, Arthur Mitchell, Raven Wilkinson, and Susan Fales-Hill, called me with congratulations. The pressure was building, but I was so elated to be getting my chance at such a seminal role that I didn't have time to be nervous.

Before kicking off our season at the Metropolitan Opera in New York, we debuted *The Firebird* on the road. Our first performances were at the Segerstrom Center for the Arts in Orange County, California. It was a homecoming; Mommy and my brothers and sisters were there. And afterward, Prince in his quiet, unassuming manner put together a small celebration for me to share in my achievement with family and friends.

Ballet blog talk praised my performance and that of Herman Cornejo's, who played the part of Prince Ivan.

"It was so good to see Herman in his solos, as he's

looking amazing," the piece read. "And Misty—her feet! her arms! her legs! her back!—was incredible. Both Herman and Misty moved through their backs, everything emanating from their center rather than a jumble of limbs being tossed about. They were fantastic apart and together, which is important for this ballet especially as they aren't supposed to be a romantic couple."

"This cast can only get better, I'm sure," the piece continued. "I can't wait to hear others' impressions of them from the Met stage."

And I was recognized as not just being technically proficient, but stylistically strong, too.

"Even though the Firebird is certainly different from Odette/Odile, Misty has the otherworldly drama and fluidity that makes me really want to see her in [Swan] Lake now. This ballet really shows [that] she's not just a technical firehouse . . . and I hope we get to see more of it soon!"

An *L.A. Times* blogged review also lifted me with its praise:

Ratmansky's revised storyline and forward-backward movement idiom finally emerged clearly with second cast leads Misty Copeland and Herman Cornejo, a hypnotizing pair. Cornejo masterfully sustained tension and contained his energy, thus giving even more force to Copeland's abandoned, creaturely performance. With them, the audience's standing ovation was absolutely spontaneous.

WE WERE BUILDING UP an incredible head of steam, garnering positive reviews and honing our performance. Our premiere on the Met's stage was drawing near.

Meanwhile, my body was giving me signals that it was being pushed past its limits.

Stress fractures are a slow injury—subtle, creeping—until they become a force that can't be ignored.

I had suffered my first serious injury my first year in the corps, when I sustained a stress fracture in my lower lumbar. At that time, I caught the hurt early. This time, I would not be so prescient.

I began to feel pain in my left shin, the leg I turn on, about six months before I made my *Firebird* debut at the Met. I had hurt myself during the relentless rehearsal process, and continued to put strain on my leg with the touring shows we were doing before debuting in New York.

The two times I performed as the Firebird in Orange County, there were moments when the pain was so strong, it seized my breath.

I tried to reason it away.

You're working out hard, practicing all day, I told myself. *Of course your leg is hurting.*

I had stopped jumping in class because I knew it would cause more damage. I saved my *grands jetés* and *petits allegros* for rehearsals and the actual shows.

But I didn't say a word about what I was feeling. In addition to my role as the Firebird, I also had the secondary lead of Gamzatti in *La Bayadère.* I feared that if I mentioned that I was in pain, I might lose one or both roles. And I wouldn't risk them, couldn't lose them.

This is for the little brown girls.

At the same time that I was working out to the point of exhaustion and trying to push fears about my weakening leg to the back of my mind, I was also having a difficult time with the ballet mistress helping me to prepare for *La Bayadère*.

Natalia Makarova was a legendary dancer who was a prima ballerina with the Kirov Ballet before she defected from Russia, later becoming a principal with ABT. I was pushed through a process that wasn't normal for ABT. I was put in a position to compete for a role with another dancer. It was clear Kevin wanted me to have the role of Gamzatti, but he told me that I would be seen by Natalia over the course of a week and it was unlikely I would get the part because she was leaning toward another dancer.

The process was intense and grueling. I knew that Natalia had issues with my body—my breasts, my weight—and did not want me featured in a ballet she was setting. I was constantly on the verge of tears but would hold them back until I was alone in the dressing room.

I knew I had to focus, to stay *en pointe* both mentally and physically. I kept working.

This is for the little brown girls.

I got the chance to perform the part of Gamzatti in one show before my premiere as the Firebird. By then, somehow, I had been able to reach a point mentally that was so strong that I was able to do things physically that I couldn't get my body to do in rehearsals. And I was able to block out Natalia's disapproval, her criticism that I wasn't ready.

Then, it was time for me to take the Metropolitan Opera's stage as the Firebird.

The day of our New York debut, the company had a dress rehearsal. Afterward, I walked out the front doors of the Met, planning to get a quick haircut since I would be attending the post premiere gala later that night.

After being inside the theater, the bright sun felt good on my face. I breathed in New York—the cabs snaking down the avenue, the crowds of tourists and art lovers ambling by. I took comfort in my city, always there to greet me, cocooning me in its embrace.

I turned around and looked up.

It was me, in full blazing color. There was my face, head thrown back in joy, and my body exuding power and feminity as I stood *en pointe* on a twenty-four-foot advertisement, waving from the front of the Metropolitan Opera. Misty Copeland. The Firebird. The banner had been there a month, since the start of the season. But still, it moved me. My eyes filled with tears. In all my years of living in New York City, I had never seen a black woman on the facade of the Met.

∞

A FEW HOURS LATER, I was in my brilliant costume of red and gold, sitting in the dressing room at the Metropolitan Opera House.

But I no longer believed that I could pull it off. I was in pain. An incredible, searing amount of pain.

How can I dance, I thought, staring in the mirror, *if I can barely walk?*

I knew that after tonight, I wouldn't be able to dance again for a long while.

Tonight, knowing that so many people had come out to support me, knowing my struggles and the significance of this moment, would have to be enough. No matter what happened on the stage, I reminded myself that there was a bigger purpose than my personal achievement.

It was time. I rose and walked toward the stage.

I was so far away from San Pedro, so different from the nineteen-year-old girl who first timidly stepped onto the Metropolitan Opera House stage, awestruck and uncertain.

Now I was a soloist, about to play a principal role in an iconic ballet for one of the most respected classical dance companies in the world. People who had nurtured me, supported me, were here, as well as others who had never before seen a professional ballet but were drawn by my presence. They were all waiting expectantly in the darkness.

My lower leg throbbed, but not as hard as my heart. I ignored both. This is what I had spent years longing for. It was time to push through. I paused in the wings before my first entrance.

The chandeliers rose, the orchestra began to play, and the lights shone down.

I was transformed. For the next ninety minutes, I fluttered and darted. I was the Firebird. There were *jetés,* and *piqués,* and *fouettés.*

And I felt no pain. All the training, all the practicing, all the nurturing had come together for this climactic moment.

"This is a *brisé*." I heard Lola de Ávila whispering in my ear.

"You are God's child." I remembered, hearing Cindy.

"You were meant to be on the stage, Misty," Mommy said in my memory of my first performance, singing "Mr. Postman" behind my brother Chris.

They were all there with me. And so many more.

This is for the little brown girls.

There were times during my performance that the applause was so loud I could barely hear the music. Then it was over.

The cast carried me, the Firebird, so that she could float away. The audience was on its feet. Shouts of "Bravo" rained down. I couldn't see their tears, but I heard that many in the audience cried tears of joy, as they danced along with me on that stage.

I accepted my bouquet of flowers, let the applause wash over me. Then I turned and left the stage numb to the pain that would come back with a flood of debilitating force two days later, when the last of my adrenaline wore off.

AFTER THE PERFORMANCE, THERE was a party on the stage to celebrate Kevin McKenzie's twentieth anniversary as ABT's director. I was joined there by many friends and supporters.

We took photographs, and for days after, the congratulatory e-mails and notes poured in.

"You have made it. You are officially a ballerina! You have proven yourself in such extreme roles as Gamzatti, then Firebird. I'm so proud of you. You have more than I ever did but I can still see when someone is the real deal. You are the epitome of all a ballerina is." So read a note from my mentor and idol, Raven Wilkinson.

"There are but so many special moments in our lives and last night was indeed one of them. . . . What joy to watch Misty on that stage!! What pride to share in her amazing accomplishment and historic performance." So wrote the president of Black Entertainment Television, Debra Lee.

"Tonight, it was as if you handed each of us—young girls and big girls—a set of wings," said the writer Veronica Chambers.

I had also received kind words about my performance as Gamzatti. My ballet mistress, Makarova, so hard on me during rehearsals, was effusive with her praise.

"Hearing the applause when the veil is removed from my head, I felt confident and in control," I wrote in my journal. "Kevin was pleased, Makarova was ecstatic. [She] said I rose to the occasion and did everything she has been asking for. *Firebird* was an incredible success. The night was huge and beyond me."

I was overwhelmed by the love and support I felt from the black community and also from so many of the ABT staffers, my peers, and the critics.

The New Yorker's Joan Acocella wrote an amazing review:

> A Firebird has to be like a bird, but to move us she also has to be like a human being. That didn't happen until the second night, when the role passed from Osipova to Misty Copeland, an A.B.T. soloist. Copeland is the only highly placed African American woman in ballet in the city. Now they should promote her for artistic reasons as well as political ones. She deserves it.

For such a highly regarded publication to say I had proven myself artistically and shown all that I was and could be was lovely affirmation. I was blown away.

I was also nearly overwhelmed a few days after my performance as the Firebird when I sat at dinner with friends and giants from the ballet world. At the table were Arthur Mitchell, former dancer Lorraine Graves, Dance Theatre of Harlem's resident choreographer, Robert Garland, and my friend Vernon, who works with ABT.

At that dinner, Arthur, who had called me on the phone to tell me how proud he was after seeing my performance in *La Bayadère* as well as in *The Firebird,* said that I had arrived. That I was a queen. That I was a *ballerina.*

He went on and on, about how I had a fire inside of me that he had not known I contained, and how I had the ability, the talent, to soar beyond anyone dancing beside me in ABT.

"You are beautiful," he said. "You have the lines, the technique, the body. You are classy and smart. You have the total package, which few have. You can have any role you desire. You have no limits."

I sat there, humbled and grateful. I thought about how I needed to recognize how special these moments were and how fortunate I was, instead of constantly worrying about what hurdle might come next. I thought about how my hard work was paying off in such sweet ways.

Still, it was difficult for me simply to bask in it all. In a way, in my mind, I was ever the latecomer, ever the student, ever the shy little girl just trying to please.

That's why it was so easy for me, standing on the crest, achieving *ballon* from the words and passion that followed my performances in *The Firebird* and *La Bayadère,* to be deflated by a few words of negativity.

And to come crashing down.

After that wonderful dinner with Arthur, Lorraine, and so many others, I went home, turned on my computer, and read a blogger's review, which criticized my Gamzatti.

Even worse, it went on to say that I didn't deserve to be a principal and it would be wrong for ABT to give me such a promotion merely to appear more racially diverse and inclusive.

It was awful. Sitting there, I couldn't believe, after all my hard work and my much praised performances, that I still had to fight this battle. And I knew that this writer was expressing what some in the audience were also, very likely, thinking.

Then I got angry. And with my anger came determination. I realized that it might take more than one stellar season, but deep down I knew that I would continue to grow, learn, and explore opportunities for more classical leading roles. Yes, I was black. And yes, I also deserved to be promoted, to stand center stage.

I had briefly allowed a negative, close-minded few to drown out all the support and love that was lifting me up. But I recovered. I had to face the truth that there were some whom I would never win over. And if I were ever promoted to principal, the negativity would likely only increase. I had to hang on to my special moments and keep fighting.

Little did I know that I was about to wage a battle on an entirely different front.

"SO WHERE DO I begin."

It was June 22, 2012, a Friday, when I sat down to my journal. Five days earlier, I had pulled out of the entire Met season.

That glorious night was the one and only time that I would be the Firebird in New York. It was only a week before that I'd taken the stage, but it felt like a lifetime.

A couple days after that performance, I was in so much pain that I finally had to admit that something was terribly wrong. Since my first serious injury a decade before, I had suffered stress fractures on several occasions. I was prone to them because my knees—those knees that bent backward—were hyperextended. That meant that when I was *en pointe*, I was putting more pressure on the front of my shin than was normal.

When I first went to the Lauridsen Ballet Centre, Diane would have me repeat the most basic of positions and moves over and over again to make sure I articulated them perfectly. At times I hated her for it, feeling as though there was no way of achieving the perfection she clearly expected. I came to understand that the constant repetition was her way of saving me. I was so flexible, I was more prone to injury, and she wanted me to do everything correctly so that I didn't hurt myself.

I'd had injuries over the years and had always healed.

But this time was more serious. I had six stress fractures in my tibia, the larger bone below the knee. I had been in pain the entire six months I had prepared for *The Firebird* and *La Bayadère*, unknowingly building fracture upon fracture.

I was devastated. I had dealt with so much emotional and psychological pressure during my career, struggling to maintain courage and confidence despite the criticism of some who did not feel a girl with my skin color or body type could ever truly belong, a life of highs closely followed by the deepest of lows.

I had started the season by seeing my face on a banner, rustling in the breeze as it hung in front of the Met. For a moment, I, a black woman, was the face of ABT. Then during my premiere performances in New York, the audience was filled with luminaries, the legends of black ballet, who deserved the applause that I received on their behalf. It was amazing.

Now this.

Having to sit out the season, the season in which I had been the Firebird and Gamzatti, was too much to bear. I felt as if everything that truly mattered to me in my life was gone.

My doctor said that I would need major surgery. And when the casting continued to be posted for the remainder of the spring season, it was as if I'd never existed. One minute you are the star, and then you are hurt. Someone moves into your light, and you disappear so completely, you cannot even find your shadow.

I put my heartache to paper.

"I just don't know how much stronger I can be and for how much longer," I confessed in my diary. I'd worked with integrity, pushing myself at a pace that sometimes felt impossible to maintain, and finally gotten a break. "I'm grateful for what I do have, but sad that it's not enough," I wrote in my journal. "God, when will it ever be easy?"

OF COURSE, IT WILL never be easy.

In life, like in ballet, you have to find your balance. To push yourself as far as you can go, but know when to pull back from the brink—of injury, of despair. I wanted to run away, but where would I go? How could I go?

I wanted to be an inspiration, but I also wanted so much more. I wanted to be a prima ballerina.

I knew that I just didn't have it in me to give up, even if I sometimes felt like a fool for continuing to believe.

Chapter 14

∝

MY SURGERY TOOK PLACE on October 10, 2012. Seven months later, I returned to the stage.

During the time that I was rehabilitating, I started taking private floor barre classes, healing with what is known as the barre à terre technique created by Boris Kniaseff. I had befriended Marjorie Liebert, the instructor, after I pulled out of the spring season. Marjorie was my savior. She kept my mind and spirit positive, while I looked toward healing. In those darkest of moments, I felt lost and without purpose. I stopped appreciating my body. Without ballet, who was I? But during rehabilitation, Marjorie convinced me to do everything I could to learn about and from my injury. That process helped me to hold on to the hopes of returning to the stage better than before—even though I still couldn't walk.

Marjorie would come to my apartment on the Upper West Side of Manhattan and I would roll out of bed and onto the floor. I had just had my cast removed and I couldn't walk, so I would do a ballet barre lying on my stomach, back, and side. She kept me focused on the things I could control. I worked on my *port de bras,* to continue to challenge myself and refine the small nuances that make a ballerina a ballerina, the fine and effortless way she carries her arms.

A month after my operation, I put my pointe shoes back on for the first time, to keep all the tiny muscles in my feet articulate, even though I wasn't yet able to stand on my toes.

I remembered the first time I'd put them on, how exhilarated I had been, and how Cindy had marveled that I could stand *en pointe* mere months after I'd discovered ballet.

Unable to do now what I had so quickly been able to do then was devastating, and having injury impact my life so late into my professional career was the most frustrating part. But Marjorie reminded me that my injury was temporary. She told me I had so much more dancing to do and not to give up my goals or my dreams. Her words were a balm in themselves, and they motivated me to reassess and adjust my technique so that I could work my flexible body more efficiently, and hopefully prevent another serious injury in the future.

I have been a dancer now for seventeen years, but I don't think I have ever focused as much on my body and my craft as I did during the months I spent healing from my latest injury.

From the moment I woke up to the moment I laid my head down at night, my everything was given to healing and strengthening.

I reported to my surgeon every three weeks to get X-rays taken. I was seeing my masseuse and acupuncturist once a week to have my muscles kneaded and bolstered. I started private gyrotonics classes that allowed me to regain strength in my legs using machines. I could emulate jumping while lying on my back, without the stress of my body weight.

Five months after undergoing major surgery on my shin, I was back rehearsing with ABT. Two months after that, I was back onstage in the ballet *Don Quixote*, premiering the principal role of the Dryad Queen.

I would be lying if I didn't admit that it was too soon. I was not "on my leg." I wasn't even close.

I read a critique of my performance.

"Misty Copeland has absolutely no jump," the writer said.

It hurt, especially because jumps have been my strength for so long. I was not yet leaping regularly in class, and it was during the actual performance that I really pushed for the first time and tried to achieve my *grands jetés.*

I performed far below my ability.

Perhaps the hardest part of my journey to healing has been recovering in the spotlight, in front of hundreds of people, presenting what I know is not my best, though it is my best for that moment. To be onstage getting criticism from people who don't know about my injury or don't care to know is difficult. And so is knowing that there may be a balletomane seeing me dance for the first time, and basing his or her impressions of me on a performance that is much less than what I am capable of.

But that is a responsibility I took on when I made the decision to step back onstage.

I definitely felt pressure to get back, to try again, from myself, from my fans, and from ABT. It's a tough position to be in. You need and want to heal completely, but you also don't want to be out for too long, to be forgotten, to miss out on roles, to lose your moment.

Knowing that some writers will be hypercritical, there are those who wonder why I bother reading reviews at all. It's true that they can be brutal, subjective, and incredibly one-sided. For all its athleticism, ballet is not a sport. There is no pure, clean way to judge it. A *jeté* is not the same as a touchdown, a *plié* not the same as a home run.

One reviewer will say you were marvelous, while another, judging the same performance, will pick out your myriad flaws. Or you notice that when it comes to a particular dancer, the reviews seem always to glow, no matter how he or she performs.

But I believe that I can learn from critiques, however biased or unfairly negative some may be. I choose to see the range of people's opinions as a way to improve. If I notice, for instance, that ten people have a negative opinion about the way I hold my arms, I will apply a laser focus to making my carriage, my *port de bras*, better. And of course, hearing the same critique from Kevin seals the deal.

I recall reading a quote in which Kevin said that my arms had yet to catch up to the ability and articulation of my legs and feet. It was hard to hear, but I was determined from then on to make my arms my best quality. I now think that my upper body, *port de bras*, and artistry have become my best qualities as a dancer, surpassing the flexible feet, pretty lines, nimble movement, and fluid coordination that come to me naturally.

I also believe that my stamina has finally clicked in just the last three or four years. Like my start in ballet, my endurance probably came later to my career than it appeared for most other dancers. But now, when I'm exhausted, I feel I'm still strong enough to keep my feet and legs in the proper positions, while before I would often lose the crispness in my lower body. As I always say, there is no shortcut in ballet technique. You repeat and repeat to get whatever you are trying to master to become second nature, for it to become as instinctive as walking. Then you can start to run.

I'm finally running.

I can more easily dismiss critiques when I know I have achieved visible improvement in whatever move or step I've attempted to fine-tune. I know at that point that I've done what I can do, and I simply can't please everyone. It is enough for me to make my best effort at achieving the perfection that is nearly impossible to attain, but that is ever the goal of a professional ballerina.

⁖

BEFORE PULLING OUT OF the Met season, and throughout my recovery, I was able to take advantage of the many amazing opportunities that have come my way beyond ABT's stage. I shot a calendar that celebrated ballet, with the wonderful photographer Gregg Delman. I became one of several athletes and artists featured in a series of commercials for Diet Dr Pepper. I have continued to hold master classes for budding ballerinas, and I'm an ambassador for the Boys and Girls Club, my other childhood home.

My extracurricular endeavors, beyond ballet or ABT, have been misunderstood by some. I also know that there are many within the ballet world who do not approve of my mainstream appeal or my passion to bring ballet to the masses and especially to underprivileged communities. Like that blogger who spoke negatively about my performances with Prince, as well as some of my other endeavors, I get criticized for "letting people in." It's almost as if ballet is this exclusive secret society that's terrified of change, even as it constantly looks for a way to stay relevant and alive. But I want everyone to feel that they could be a part of my world, if they want to be.

My goal has been to share ballet with an audience that might otherwise not know or appreciate it. Of course, not every budding dancer will be fortunate enough to have a Liz Cantine as her drill instructor, spotting her potential, or a Cindy who takes her expertise to a working-class neighborhood, then offers a free education to the most ambitious talents. But that doesn't mean we can't make a start. Recently, I helped facilitate the founding of ABT's Project Plié, a partnership between the company and the Boys and Girls Clubs of America that will formalize the process that introduced me to ballet, bringing ABT-trained teachers to clubs across the country to scout for talented kids who might otherwise never set foot on a stage. They'll learn history and dance theory, and be provided with scholarships to hone their talents. And as the figurehead for the program, I'll get to embody the incredible symbolism that being different can stand for. I am different and I accept it. I'm aware of the power that it holds in opening doors for others who are underprivileged or underrepresented—it's a power that goes far beyond me or any of my individual achievements.

I am not just trying to shepherd and mentor new dancers. I also feel deeply that there is a huge, untapped audience of ballet viewers. And among disadvantaged children, or children of color who are often not exposed to this art form, I believe that ballet provides much to learn. Studies show that dancers have a very high rate of success in any endeavor they pursue because of the poise and discipline, both physical and mental, that they must develop practicing their craft. Those are valuable attributes for anyone to possess. But children cannot develop them if they are not exposed to dance. I am willing to carry that message and pass on those lessons even as I realize I may not see immediate change in my lifetime.

But when all is said and done, it is standing on the stage, articulating ballet's majesty, that is and has always been my first and strongest love.

∞

I LOVE THAT IMAGE of the Firebird.

It exemplifies the most joyful moments in the life of a dancer. The exhilaration of performance, the ecstasy of losing yourself in movement. But those moments are fleeting. In between, there are hours of grueling practice, and days, weeks, even months of despair when injuries or other problems keep you from performing your best. Or from dancing at all.

When I was recuperating from my shin injury, I had a great deal of time for reflection. I often contemplated whether or not I would—or should—dance again. Did I have a different path and purpose going forward? Perhaps I had gone as far as I could, and from now on, my role would be to encourage and inspire as a mentor rather than as a dancer.

But now that I'm back onstage, having grown in ways I didn't realize were possible, I know that I'm here to do both.

No matter how many hours I devote to practice, no matter

how much of my life I give to ballet, the work never stops. Every dancer knows that there will always be someone younger and better waiting in the wings to take her place. The older you get, the less you are physically capable of. Yet age and experience give your art depth and complexity, and I am so excited to continue to grow and explore. It's all about finding that balance.

I still worry, far more than I should, about what the ballet world thinks of me—whether I will ever be accepted and seen as the talent I was once praised for as a prodigy, a well-rounded artist deserving of respect. Or will I forever be "the black ballerina," an oddity who doesn't quite compare?

But in my moments of clarity I envision all those people whose lives have been touched by my story and my accomplishments so far, who upon seeing my journey know that you can start late, look different, be uncertain, and still succeed.

My fears are that it could be another two decades before another black woman is in the position that I hold with an elite ballet company. That if I don't rise to principal, people will feel I have failed them.

I still want it. To be a principal dancer with ABT, to be Nikiya in *La Bayadère*, Juliet to a soaring Romeo, Odette and Odile in *Swan Lake*, and Giselle. But whether or not I become the first female African American principal dancer in an elite company, I know that I've had an impact by having a voice and sharing my story.

There's another image of the Firebird that I love: how she emerges triumphant, and then soars into the sky, like the phoenix rising from the ashes.

I've come so far from that first class I took in my baggy

gym clothes. I know that by being here, for seventeen years, in this rarefied, difficult, elitist, beautiful world, I have made my mark in history and ballet. I will forever fight, performing as if it's my last show.

And I will love every minute of it.

THERE'S ONE QUESTION I'VE been asked most often since becoming the first African American principal dancer at ABT. So, what's next?

I know what these well-meaning fans, journalists, and friends expect me to say. They want to hear about TV appearances, guest roles on Broadway, prime-time competition hosting gigs, my writing, even film projects. They want to hear about the trappings of modern celebrity that seem so glamorous to outsiders.

But most often, when I'm asked about my plans for the future, I shrug and smile, then say, "Rehearsal."

Promotion announcements happen randomly, and there's no set structure to them, but it's fitting that I found out about my promotion in the studio where I've spent so much time over the last decades since joining ABT's studio company in 2000. I was promoted to soloist at twenty-four, but that was a quieter affair. Kevin had called me into his office toward the end of that year's spring season and shared the happy news, but it was all secret: I couldn't tell anyone until he made the announcement at our company meeting and a press release went out.

When I found out that I would become a principal, though, it was in front of my closest colleagues: the dancers who have seen me during every injury, through every difficult step of new choreography, through every round of warm-up pliés, through each new role. It felt fitting that I found out in the midst of the company—my company.

There is a video of that moment taken by Julie Kent, a thirty-year veteran of ABT who had danced her last performance just a few nights before. I had no idea she was filming, and you could tell. In it, I'm flopped on the floor wearing no makeup, looking just like I would any given morning before rehearsal. The news was a complete surprise. As I heard Kevin say "Misty, take a bow," Jennifer Whalen, one of my best friends, kisses me on the cheek. I'm smiling—you can't imagine how filled with joy I was in that moment—but as soon as I lifted my head from Jennifer's black leotard–clad shoulder, my face crumpled into tears. How else could I react when my biggest dream came true?

It's been several years since I began work on Life in Motion, but just because I published a memoir, it doesn't mean I have all the answers about myself. I've been open about how my childhood was the beginning of a difficult quest for stability. Being one of a boisterous group of siblings and feeling rootless and unmoored as we moved from place to place has always made me crave acceptance and balance. As I traveled the country dancing and speaking, I've been amazed to see just how much people have connected with and related to me. As different as I felt during my childhood, with all of its accompanying struggles and blessings, it's been wonderful to see that there are so many people out there going through very similar things. It's a comforting feeling that's made me feel more at ease and accept a lot about myself, both I as am now and as I was in the past.

In some ways, I wish I hadn't been the one to achieve this dream. It means so much to me to see wonderful black ballerinas who came before me, who faced so much more adversity, receiving the honor they are due. One of my favorite interviews in the months before I was promoted was with a travel magazine that ran an article on Raven Wilkinson's role as a mentor in my life.

My entire career has been devoted to becoming an ABT principal because I wanted to break a barrier that often seemed so insurmountable. Despite what some have suggested, personal fame is not my goal. Yes, I wanted to make history, but it was never on my own behalf. By becoming the first black woman to hold such a role in a national company, I could take a step forward for all the beautiful young dancers who will come after me. I want to pave the way for them, because I hope it will make their journeys easier. I even pray that they will surpass me, if only because it will mean that their burdens have been lightened and they can leap forward into the spotlight. I hope that young dancers, in companies all around the country, will have to face fewer questions on whether they belong in ballet, both from others and in their own minds, whether that is because of their size, shape, or skin color. My message remains the same: if there is space for a quiet little brown girl from San Pedro in ballet, there is room for you, too.

I was off the night of my promotion, but I went straight

into rehearsal after the meeting to prepare for my role of the Autumn Fairy in Cinderella the next evening. And the next morning, I was back at the barre, where I have always found so much comfort and inspiration. To the outside world, I was different, but I felt like who I've always been—a ballerina, striving to do her best at what she loves.

Acknowledgments

I NEVER THOUGHT THAT I would be so blessed as to be given the opportunity to share all that makes me *me*: my dreams, my struggles, and my hope to inspire many to dare to dream bigger than they can imagine.

I have to thank my family for the strength we have maintained throughout our lives. Erica, Doug, Chris, Lindsey, and Cameron: it was our belief in one another and ourselves that made it possible to beat and defy all odds. Thank you, Mom, for not giving up. Thank you, Daddy, for stepping into my life and raising me as your own. Cindy, Wolf, and Patrick: What can I say other than that I'm not sure where my life would be without our fateful meeting. Thank you for taking me into your home without judgment . . . just genuine love. Thank you for bringing me to ballet! I will forever be grateful. Thank you, Liz and Dick, my godparents. Thank you for not only being the catalysts to my career but for remaining a part of my life: for your guidance and love.

Boys and Girls Club of San Pedro! Boys and Girls Clubs of America! Everything you stand for is real, and it *works*. You change lives and started my future, and what a future it has become!

American Ballet Theatre: thank you for the endless belief and support in me. I'm proud to be an ABT baby. From the summer intensive to the Studio Company to a member of the main company! Thank you for helping to create an atmosphere where I felt capable of being a new mold for what a ballerina can be! To Susan, my second mommy, I can't say enough. Your mentorship changed my views and mind-set. You have set the bar high. Vicky! I think you were one of the first brown ballerinas I ever met. Thank you for taking the time to show me that I'm not alone, and for being an incredible example that my dreams are limitless. Diane, the short time spent training at the Lauridsen Ballet Centre was so vital to my training. Thank you for *never* taking it easy on me, for never treating me any differently from your other students, and for pushing me beyond what I thought my limits were. Raven, you gave me that second wind, inspiring me not to feel sorry for myself and my situation, but to fight for what I know is right. You remind me every day that life isn't easy, and therefore the fight in me is that much fiercer. Your perseverance is beyond admirable. You will always be that example of what a true ballerina is! Marjorie, I don't have to say it, because we both know it. We speak the same language, and your knowledge is endless. I admire and respect you, and I am grateful for the discoveries I have started to uncover within myself and my body because of you.

Gilda, where would I be without you? Vernon's introduction brought forth this magical collaboration that neither of us knew could reach these heights. And boy, do we have so much higher to go! Thank you for your incredible vision and for bringing it to life. You've brought ballet to a level I wasn't sure was possible. To the team at Touchstone/Simon & Schuster, Megan Reid, and Steve Troha: Who would have thought . . . well, you guys did! And it's all happening. Thank you for the tremendous work and belief! Charisse, what a beautiful experience this has been, to sit in my living room and talk to a friend. This book has been far from work. It has been an exploration of myself, my past, and my future. Your words have brought it to life!

And last but not least: O. Our relationship has been more than I could have ever dreamed of it becoming. You have been my biggest fan, my voice of reason, and always good for a debate when that's needed. Thank you for being here always, and for helping me to believe that brown ballerinas could benefit from seeing and hearing my story and for encouraging me to be a mentor.

Index

Index

277

Index

Life in Motion

When thirteen-year-old Misty Copeland first walks into a ballet class at the Boys and Girls Club in San Pedro, California, she has no idea that it will change her world. Her chaotic home life, filled with five siblings and her mother's changing husbands and boyfriends, is in stark contrast to the control, beauty, and grace Misty experiences in ballet. A seeming ugly duckling, with a small head, sloping shoulders, and big feet, Misty learns that she has the ideal body for ballet. She has the uncanny ability to copy complex steps perfectly. *Life in Motion* is Misty's personal account of her journey to become the first African American soloist at the prestigious American Ballet Theatre (ABT) in more than twenty years. Misty relates the challenges she faced, from living on food stamps to a bitter, highly publicized custody battle between her mother and her dance teacher. Through it all, Misty remains true to herself and committed to her goal. Her remarkable story will inspire anyone struggling against seemingly insurmountable obstacles. Misty Copeland is proof positive that with perseverance, dedication, and a little bit of luck, dreams can come true.

1. Misty contrasts her shyness to the confidence she feels dancing and performing. Of her childhood she says, "I felt awkward, like I didn't fit in anywhere, and I lived in constant fear of letting my mother down, or my teachers, or myself." How do you think her introverted personality affects her as a performer? Can anxiety become a strength, rather than a weakness? How does she learn to cope with it?

2. Misty's relationships with the male figures in her life often bring her strength. Misty describes her wonderful relationship with Harold, her mother's third husband. As she says, "Memories of Harold are never cloudy, only clear and bright." Her relationship with Olu brings her strength and confidence, especially in finding her place at ABT and becoming a mentor to others. Why do you think these influences are powerful for her? Can you contrast them with the less-positive legacy of her mother's other husbands and boyfriends?

3. Misty finds support and encouragement from ballet teacher Cindy Bradley, who invites Misty to leave her mother's meager, overcrowded apartment to live with the Bradley family. What could Cindy provide Misty that her mother could not? In what ways does Misty connect with other maternal or supportive figures after she leaves the Bradleys?

4. Misty has a complex relationship with her mother: "I love my mother, but I've never really understood her." Their relationship is taxed to the breaking point when Misty's mother forces her to leave the Bradleys and return home. Eventually Misty withdraws her petition to become a legally emancipated minor, which Cindy helped her request. Do you think this was entirely Misty's decision? How did this painful process affect Misty's dancing career? Her relationship with her mother?

5. Misty's childhood was one of intermittent poverty and rootlessness. Her mother was continually running away from bad situations. How did this affect the way Misty dealt with obstacles later in life?

6. Consider Misty's many experiences with prejudice. Her mother's fourth husband, Robert, displayed a penchant for abusive racial epithets, and Misty also finds bigotry pervasive in the world of ballet, where she must often paint her face lighter for performances. To what degree do you think racism has affected Misty's career as a dancer? What have her experiences taught her?

7. Did Misty's discussion of the myth of eating disorders and ballet surprise you? Discuss that and any other preconceived notions you may have had about ballet before reading this book. Which were dispelled? Which were proven accurate?

8. When discussing her friend and fellow dancer Eric Underwood, Misty wonders if what led them both to dance was serendipity or destiny. Which do you think it was for Misty? What does Misty seem to believe?

9. Misty says, "Mommy had always been afraid that I'd given up my childhood for a dream." Do you think she did? If so, was it worth it?

10. Misty admits to being a perfectionist since childhood. By the end of the book, how does Misty come to terms with the idea of perfection?

11. To this day, ABT has never had an African American principal dancer. What do you think of Misty's campaign to be the first?

12. The book begins and ends with Misty's dancing the role of the Firebird. What is the significance of the Firebird, both her performance and the character, to Misty?

A Conversation
with Misty Copeland

In the book you are very candid about the struggles of your early childhood. Do you think those experiences were a help or a hindrance to your determination to become a ballerina?

They were absolutely a help. You need perseverance, determination, and drive to succeed in the ballet world. All of my faults and insecurities as a child were highlighted by ballet and it pushed me to prove myself despite them. In the end, wanting to please people, striving for perfection, even survival, are all attributes a ballerina needs to have.

In addition to your work with ABT, you also have worked with Prince, judged a national TV dance competition, had a viral TV campaign for a sportswear brand, signed a film deal, and worked with the President's Council on Fitness, Sports and Nutrition, which helped introduce ballet to a wider audience. What kind of results are you seeing from helping to make this art form more popular and democratic?

The most impressive is seeing a more diverse audience at the Metropolitan Opera House. That is *huge* for ballet, as well as seeing a ton of brown ballerinas willing to step into this secluded world because they can see spaces for themselves now.

You express a great deal of affection for New York City from almost the moment you arrived for ABT's summer intensive program. Do you still feel the same way about it?

I feel the same. The yearning I felt while away from NYC as an adolescent is a bit less dramatic now. I'm always happy to be home here, but I don't feel as though I'm missing out on the fast-paced energy and growth of the city as I once did when I was on tour.

Many of your awards and accomplishments in ballet are even more remarkable because you are often the first African American to achieve them. In what ways do you think the world of ballet is changing for future performers? For the audience?

I think it will be after my retirement from ballet that I will realize the weight put on me by being the first. I am so "in it" now, and focused on the challenges of becoming what I need to be from day to day, that I don't float above myself and see the scarier picture of not living up to expectations. But things are changing daily. It's exciting. To see myself reflected in the younger generation of ballet dancers helps give me hope.

Although they are both art forms, ballet and writing are extremely different. Did you enjoy the writing experience? Were there any particular challenges for you?

I really enjoyed it. I've always enjoyed writing in journals. It was my way of expressing myself before I really knew how to speak up for myself more publicly, so the whole experience was very cathartic. The most challenging part for me was letting go of the story and putting it out into the world, and also giving Charisse Jones, my coauthor, the freedom to do what she does and just help me write! It was scary to trust someone with my life story.

In the book you confess the very human tendency to focus on the rare negative comment or criticism amid a sea of praise. Did you read the reviews for your book? How did your experiences with reviews for your performances affect the way you handled your book reviews?

If anything I'm even more prepared for my book reviews because I've experienced those performance reviews. The book stuff is a bit different in that these are my life experiences, so it's hard to imagine someone would judge or critique another person's life experiences by any objective measure. It's another thing to be a part of a subjective art form where you have to be thick-skinned enough to handle criticism. But to have someone place judgment on a life they've never personally lived is strange.

In addition to this memoir, you've also written a children's book. What stories do you dream of telling next?

The history of minorities, especially brown people, in the classical ballet world. I want to share my experiences in this unique setting as well as undiscovered and untold stories of generations of stories before me.

This book was a national bestseller, and while on tour, you had the opportunity to engage with many of your fans one-on-one. What advice or insight would you like to leave your readers that you might not have addressed in this memoir's pages?

That I'm nowhere near the be-all and end-all for ballet. I just want to spark interest in an unlikely audience and to bring awareness and education to those who may not otherwise feel welcomed.

Enhance Your Book Club

1. Get into the spirit of things: find a local ballet studio and attend a recital, or even take a beginner's class. Many schools offer classes for adult novices. If you have questions about ballet, there are many helpful Internet sites. ABT's website offers a dictionary of ballet terms, some with video illustrations (http://www.abt.org/education/dictionary/). Britain's Royal Ballet has uploaded many videos on ballet steps and terms and the history of ballet; see https://www.youtube.com/playlist?list=PL7E40E6 E2DAB561B5 and https://www.youtube.com/playlist ?list=PLFEuShFvJzBww3lVbFABGB0HbIxNQ2TiA.

2. Have the members of your group talk about any early experiences with the arts—dance lessons, musical instrument classes, visual arts lessons, etc.—then compare your experiences. Is any member of your group still practicing his or her art? Discuss what art added to your lives.

3. Misty had a wonderful, supportive experience with the Boys and Girls Club, and she continues to help promote their causes. Visit the organization's website, www.bgca.org, to find out more about the clubs, to locate one in your area, and even to have the opportunity to volunteer at the club. Next, visit http://www.abt.org/education/projectplie/bgca/ to learn about Project Plié, the Boys and Girls Club's partnership with ABT to "introduce ballet to a broad array of children by conducting educational and activity-based master classes in member clubs across the United States."